BEFORE
HOLLYWOOD

BEFORE HOLLYWOOD

Turn-of-the-Century American Film

Texts by Jay Leyda and Charles Musser.
Additional texts by John L. Fell, Stephen Gong, Neil Harris, Richard Koszarski, Judith Mayne, Brooks McNamara, Russell Merritt, Alan Trachtenberg

Hudson Hills Press, New York
in Association with the American Federation of Arts

This book has been published in conjunction with the film exhibition *Before Hollywood: Turn-of-the-Century Film from American Archives*, which was organized by the American Federation of Arts. The film exhibition has been supported by the National Endowment for the Arts, the National Endowment for the Humanities, the New York State Council on the Arts, the Eugene and Estelle Ferkauf Foundation, the Arthur Ross Foundation, and the Brown Foundation, Inc., and by Hilva Landsman, Barbara Goldsmith and Frank Perry, and James Ottaway, Jr.

Published in the United States by Hudson Hills Press, Inc., Suite 1308, 230 Fifth Avenue, New York, NY 10001-7704.

Distributed in the United States, its territories and possessions, Mexico, and Central and South America by Rizzoli International Publications, Inc.
Distributed in Canada by Irwin Publishing Inc.
Distributed in the United Kingdom, Eire, Europe, Israel, and the Middle East by Phaidon Press Limited.
Distributed in Japan by Yohan (Western Publications Distribution Agency).

Editor and Publisher: Paul Anbinder
Copy editor: Martina D'Alton
Designer: Steven Schoenfelder
Composition: Trufont Typographers, Inc.
Manufactured in Hong Kong.

Library of Congress No. 86-72687
ISBN 0-933920-91-1

Contents

Acknowledgments

I am particularly pleased to write these introductory remarks to the catalogue that accompanies *Before Hollywood: Turn-of-the-Century Film from American Archives*. There has never been as extensive a film exhibition devoted exclusively to the early accomplishments of the American cinema, and certainly not one in which titles were drawn from virtually every major film collection in this country: the American Film Institute Collection at the Library of Congress, the International Museum of Photography at George Eastman House, the Library of Congress, the Museum of Modern Art, and the UCLA Film Archives. We wish to express our sincere thanks to these film archives for their cooperation and participation throughout the planning and implementation of *Before Hollywood*. The AFA is proud to have played such an important role in this project and to have given greater exposure to the important cinematic works painstakingly acquired and preserved by our film archives.

The *Before Hollywood* project was first proposed to us in the early 1980s by AFA Film Program Director Sam McElfresh. It was his enthusiasm and serious commitment that persuaded us to pursue the project and his leadership that brought it to fruition. Since its inception, the curatorial and intellectual responsibility for the exhibition has been in the hands of two people: Jay Leyda, Pinewood Chair of Cinema Studies at New York University and a leading authority on American, Soviet, and Chinese film; and Charles Musser, film historian for the Thomas A. Edison Papers at Rutgers University, a scholar of the early American film industry and a prize-winning filmmaker. In addition to selecting titles for the exhibition, Professor Leyda provided his wise counsel on every aspect of the project and drafted the introduction to this catalogue. His vast knowledge and passion for the subject contributed immeasurably to the excellence of the exhibition. Dr. Musser served as co-selector with Professor Leyda, drafted one of the catalogue essays, wrote and selected materials for program notes on many titles in the exhibition, and assumed an advisory role in the preparation of the publication. He also worked closely with the film archives in negotiating the loans, helped organize the project's planning convocation, and personally restored a number of previously truncated prints especially for this exhibition. To these two, we owe a special debt of gratitude for their scholarly contributions, without which the *Before Hollywood* exhibition would not have been possible.

We are also indebted to the other six distinguished experts whose essays enliven this catalogue and make it a resource of lasting importance to the field: John L. Fell (San Francisco State University), Neil Harris (University of Chicago), Brooks McNamara (New York University), Judith Mayne (Ohio State University), Russell Merritt (University of Wisconsin-Madison), and Alan Trachtenberg (Yale University). Thanks are also extended to the many film scholars who wrote the original program notes for the sixty-nine films in the exhibition; to Richard Koszarski (American Museum of the Moving Image), who provided stills and text for the catalogue's photographic essay on early cinema production and exhibition; and to Stephen Gong (currently of the National Center for Film and Video Preservation at the American Film Institute) for his catalogue statement on film preservation.

The planning of this unique project has been particularly complex. In the early stages, Sam McElfresh worked closely with a core group of film experts to develop the concept of the exhibition and to orchestrate its initial support. For their involvement with the project, we wish to acknowledge the following: Eileen Bowser, Jon Gartenberg, and Herbert Reynolds (Museum of Modern Art); Lawrence F. Karr and Audrey E. Kupferberg (American Film Institute); George C. Pratt (George Eastman House); Robert Rosen (UCLA Film Archives); Paul C. Spehr (Library of Congress); Richard M. Gollin (University of Rochester); Janet K. Cutler (Montclair State College); Stephen Gong (National Endowment for the Arts); Sally Yerkovich (National Endowment for the Humanities); and B. Ruby Rich (New York State Council on the Arts). The dedication and generosity of these individuals—who saw the potential for *Before Hollywood*—merit special thanks.

I also wish to express my appreciation to the AFA Film Advisory Committee for its invaluable support during the formative stages of this project. The following deserve special mention: the late Willard Van Dyke who, as Committee Chairman, steadfastly championed the project; John G. Hanhardt, whose able advice and strong commitment to the exhibition ensured its premiere at the Whitney Museum of American Art; William D. Judson, a scholar of early cinema, who proved a valuable advisor to the project; and Melinda Ward, who was responsible for bringing *Before Hollywood* to the attention of the media arts community at the 1983 National Alliance of Media Arts Centers conference.

Another crucial aspect of the planning stage of *Before Hollywood* was the "Invitational Convocation on Early Cinema," held under AFA auspices in June, 1983. After co-curators Leyda and Musser selected a broad sampling of titles, prints were shipped from each of the archives to a central location—the Library of Congress—for a gathering of film scholars. On this occasion, project personnel and invited experts were given the rare chance to view twenty-five hours of the best surviving examples of America's early cinema heritage. From this experience, catalogue authors were able to write original essays grounded in a unique overview of films of the period, and the curators to refine topic areas and make their final selection of films to be included in the exhibition. Special thanks go to Paul C. Spehr of the Library of Congress for hosting this event in the newly opened Mary Pickford Theatre, and to former AFA Coordinator of Film Scheduling Marian Luntz for her organization of the ambitious convocation.

We also wish to thank AFA Film Program Assistants Sharon Doane and William O'Donnell who, assisted by AFA Coordinator of Film Circulation and Loans Fred Riedel, coordinated all production aspects of this catalogue. Original frame enlargements that illustrate the catalogue were photographed by Jan-Christopher Horak (George Eastman House), Joyce E. Jesinowski (Museum of Modern Art), Patrick G. Loughney (Library of Congress), and John Tirpak (UCLA Film Archives). We owe our appreciation to Teri Roiger for transcription of text, Martina D'Alton for editing of the catalogue, and Steven Schoenfelder for the handsome design of the publications and wall panels that accompany the exhibition.

Assembling circulating copies of the rare, fragile films that make up the *Before Hollywood* exhibition was an extremely complicated task. The responsibility for that endeavor was ably assumed by AFA Coordinators of Film Circulation and Loans Fred Riedel and Stephen Vitiello, assisted by AFA Coordinator of Scheduling Tom Smith. The generous cooperation of the many archives, film distribution companies, and film laboratories who helped create prints of the films entrusted to their care was essential to the success of this effort. Special thanks go to the following individuals and institutions who went to great trouble to provide the best possible materials for this exhibition: Robert Gitt, Charles Hopkins and William Ault (UCLA Film Archives); Peter Williamson and Charles Silver (Museum of Modern Art); John Kuiper and Allan J. Bobey (George Eastman House); Joe Empsucha (American Film Institute); Jerry Hatfield (Library of Congress); Michelle Snapes (British Film Institute); Matty Kemp (Mary Pickford Company); Nick Draklich (Republic Pictures); Theodore Ewing (Blackhawk Films); Dick May (Turner Entertainment Company); Lola E. Langer (Paramount Pictures Corporation); Karla Davidson (MGM/UA); John E. Allen, Jr. and Sean Coughlin (John E. Allen, Inc.); Film Technology Company, Inc.; and YCM Laboratory.

Philip Brunelle, artistic director and principal conductor of the Minnesota Opera Company, first made us aware of the invaluable role played by music when he provided piano accompaniment for three *Before Hollywood* titles screened at the 1983 NAMAC Conference. We are delighted that Mr. Brunelle's accomplished accompaniment will be added to 16mm circulating prints of *Before Hollywood* as a music track.

No exhibition of this scope and importance is possible without substantial financial support. From the beginning, the United States government has offered such support, particularly in the early and critical stages of the project, through major grants from the National Endowment for the Arts and the National Endowment for the Humanities. It was joined in this effort by the New York State Council for the Arts. We also wish to acknowledge the generous assistance of the following private foundations and individuals: the Eugene and Estelle Ferkauf Foundation; the Arthur Ross Foundation; the Brown Foundation, Inc.; Hilva Landsman; Barbara Goldsmith and Frank Perry; and James Ottaway, Jr. Additional support for the catalogue has been provided by the J.M. Kaplan Fund, the DeWitt Wallace Fund, and the Henry Luce Foundation through the AFA Revolving Fund for Publications.

I want to thank all those AFA staff members who have contributed so much to the realization of this project over the past six years. In particular, I wish to acknowledge Sam McElfresh, AFA Film Program Director, for his overall direction of the project; Tom Smith, Coordinator of Film Scheduling, for securing presentation sites and speakers for the national tour; Jane S. Tai, Associate Director, for her invaluable assistance in fundraising; Sandra Gilbert, Public Information Director, for her energetic publicity efforts; and past Film Program staff members Diane Kaiser Koszarski, Susan Poland, Marjorie Cohn, and Esther Samra, all of whom assisted in the organization of *Before Hollywood*.

Finally, I wish to express my appreciation to the AFA Trustees for their sustained support during the long evolution of this project. In particular, I would like to extend warm and personal thanks to Trustee Hilva Landsman. Her extraordinary commitment to the concept of *Before Hollywood* was matched by generous individual sponsorship and extremely productive fundraising efforts on behalf of the project, for which we are deeply grateful.

Wilder Green
Director
The American Federation of Arts

Introduction

In the first two decades of the cinema (1895–1915), screens throughout the United States were flooded with a wealth of experimental works as filmmakers began to explore the limits and resources of this new medium. Tragically, many of these innovative films have been lost—others survive thanks to ongoing efforts of dedicated film archivists. These rare works of the late nineteenth and early twentieth century, many of which have been recently discovered and preserved, constitute an unusually important part of American aesthetic and cultural history, but the vast majority have not been seen by either the general public or by most film scholars since their initial turn-of-the-century release.

To present today's audiences with a sampling of films from this formative period in American film history, co-curator Charles Musser and I reviewed the holdings of the five preeminent film collections in this country: the American Film Institute, the International Museum of Photography at George Eastman House, the Library of Congress, the Museum of Modern Art, and the UCLA Film Archive. We were aware of the rich examples of films from this period entrusted to their care; as well, each of these archives had increased its collection through vital attention to preservation and restoration, adding to the quantity of materials from which our choices could be made. Thankfully, all agreed on the value of a traveling exhibition of films to acquaint audiences at cultural institutions across the country with the earliest years of American filmmaking.

Several factors determined our selections for the *Before Hollywood* exhibition. We certainly wished the films to convey the same visual quality experienced by their original audiences. We also looked for the unexpected, the surprising: early American film's innovations are internationally acclaimed, but few moviegoers today know firsthand, for example, the lovely handcolored dance films enjoyed by early viewers. We included little-known examples of the work of America's most celebrated film pioneers (e.g., Edwin S. Porter, D. W. Griffith, Cecil B. DeMille), but also sought discoveries by lesser-known directors. In so doing, we felt obligated to go beyond mainstream entertainment films to explore other turn-of-the-century movie fare: news subjects, animation, trick films and comedies. We were rewarded greatly in these efforts: among the art forms that illuminate the mores, values, and conditions of an era, film is especially revealing, and many of the "little" films of the *Before Hollywood* period offer the biggest revelations. Just as the narrative elements of this popular art tell us much about the audience for which it was produced, so its photographic

qualities document the time and place in which it was made: in *The Black Hand* (Biograph, 1906), for example, immigrant values are celebrated in a drama shot with hidden cameras on the streets of Manhattan. Here are sharp observations on the attitudes and life of turn-of-the-century America. Finally, we attempted to represent as full a range of early cinema genres as possible—actualities (including documentaries and travelogues), comedies (including trick films, chase films, and animations), dramas and melodramas, and socially aimed films—from a broad sampling of production companies.

The times in which these films were made is reflected in their stories and images, and time—or most properly, production dates—determines the rough chronology of *Before Hollywood's* six programs. Beyond this, programs have been organized into topic areas of special significance to American life at that time: "clusters" that show variations on a subject (e.g., fascination with movement, patriotism, courtship and marriage, Americans at play, crime and criminals, changing perceptions of women, the frontier spirit, etc.) or method that had brought success. We attempted in this way to give some impression of these years' swift current of inventiveness and surprise that kept nickelodeon spectators coming back for more.

In the spring of 1983, as the planning for this project reached a critical phase, a group of scholars convened at the Library of Congress. They viewed films over the course of three very full days, seeing most of the selections in these final programs and many others besides. Out of these screenings and exchanges came a group of provocative essays that view American cinema from original perspectives. Focusing on specific aspects of motion picture practice, several authors traced evolving conventions and representational methods. In "Dream Visions in Pre-Hollywood Film," film historian Russell Merritt considers the ways in which dreams, as a narrative device, were used by filmmakers to break with orthodox storytelling constraints during the silent era. Co-curator Charles Musser's essay, "The Changing Status of the Film Actor," traces the film actor's changing role in the industry and status in society. "Pre-Hollywood" cinema developed in relation to many other cultural forms—the theater, vaudeville, newspapers, photography, magic lantern shows, the short story, and even painting. In his essay, "Cellulose Nitrate Roots: Popular Entertainments and the Birth of Film Narrative," film scholar John Fell surveys these borrowings, concentrating on early film's origins in the comic strip and theatrical melodrama.

The cinema's plethora of antecedents has intrigued a wide range of scholars whose main interest have been in other, often related fields. Brooks McNamara, professor of Performance Studies at New York University, draws on his knowledge of set design to examine how American pioneer filmmakers incorporated contemporary theatrical principles in "Scene Design and the Early Film," and Alan Trachtenberg, professor of American Studies at Yale University, explores the ways turn-of-the-century photographic practices, modes, and genres were applied to the cinema in "Photography/Cinematography."

The ways in which the movie-going experience affected early audiences has emerged as a central issue for today's film historians, particularly now that these films are once again available for modern audiences. Judith Mayne of the Center for Women's Studies at Ohio State University describes how women in films were presented as objects of the male gaze (the men in the audience as well as the male protagonists in the films) in "Uncovering the Female Body." Neil Harris, professor of history at the University of Chicago, argues that early cinema, an often anonymous form of technological image-making, was also, as the title of his essay states, "A Subversive Form."

It is our hope that the *Before Hollywood* project will serve as a catalyst for film preservation, restoration, and exhibition. Too often, silent films have only been available in poorly copied 16mm prints rather than in their pristine, 35mm format. This has resulted in significant loss in quality, as well as in actual loss of portions of the image as the intended framing has been altered. An archival exhibition should be available to a broad audience in the original format, something provided by *Before Hollywood*, the AFA's first touring program in 35mm, as well as carefully printed 16mm versions. Several motion pictures from the Library of Congress' Paperprint Collection were rephotographed on 35mm stock for the purpose of this tour. In several cases, participating archives returned to original nitrate materials to strike the best possible quality prints. Ironically, some films only survive in 16mm form. So, for the 35mm show, full-frame optical blow-ups of two titles were created: *The Passion Play of Oberammergau* (Edison, 1898) and *The Ruse* (New York Motion Picture Company, 1915).

Materials from various archives were also combined to produce the most complete prints possible. Thus, animated titles in *Coney Island at Night* (Edison, 1905) were drawn from Library of Congress paperprints, while that film's extraordinarily beautiful night photography comes from original Edison negatives held by the Museum of Modern Art. Two Biograph films, *The Usurer* (Biograph, 1910) and *One Is Business; the Other Crime* (Biograph, 1912), have been restored to contain their original intertitles. For *The Miller's Daughter* (Edison, 1905), a missing scene has been suggested by inserting a surviving frame enlargement and catalogue description. This permanent preservation and restoration has been a satisfying though complex undertaking requiring the coordinated efforts of several institutions. The project has been one of happy surprises, a few of which are taking form at this moment: preservation work continues as the catalogue goes to press. What will *Princess Nicotine* (Vitagraph, 1909) look like with its original color tints? When the long-lost *Blackton Sketching Edison* (Edison, 1896) is finally shown, will the drawing of Edison reproduced in this catalogue correspond to the one Blackton is sketching in the film—as the artist himself has claimed?

The five major archival collections that agreed to act as loan sources for the *Before Hollywood* project have acquired and preserved films that in and of themselves are important documents in the history of cinema, and also serve to illuminate the historical and cultural context of the period from which they emerged. Unfortunately, film preservation work can never keep pace with the rapid rate of nitrate deterioration that afflicts all films made prior to the 1950s. Thus, much of film history is rapidly disappearing, while many of those films that *have* been preserved remain unseen except by a small group of scholars and specialists. The brief films of *Before Hollywood* constitute an important, otherwise unavailable part of our cultural history, and we have been delighted to add our contribution to that of the AFA and America's archivists in bringing them to American audiences.

Jay Leyda

Saving Early Cinema

Motion pictures, among the most influential creations of modern society, are surprisingly ephemeral: more than half of the theatrical films produced in this country before 1951 have been lost forever. Photographed on nitrate (nitrocellulose) film stock, a highly unstable material, many of these films eventually deteriorated or disintegrated through chemical decomposition. Others were simply junked so that film studios, wary of this hazardous material (nitrate film is also highly flammable), could save on storage costs. Significantly, early cinema was disposed of because it was *seen as* a disposable product by its creators and audiences: regarded as "mere entertainment" for mass audiences and without the pedigree accorded to unique art objects, movies were not considered worthy of collection or preservation. It has taken many years for our culture to recognize the richness and value of its film heritage. Today, film archivists across the country are actively engaged in the complex and costly task of film preservation. Still, much of their work remains unseen outside the walls of the archives. The American Federation of Arts' *Before Hollywood* exhibition provides contemporary audiences their first opportunity to view dozens of films from the earliest period of American cinema and to celebrate the dedicated archivists responsible for saving these gems for future generations.

A number of institutions deserve recognition for their ongoing work in safeguarding our film history. The Library of Congress, legal depository of films registered for copyright, accepted its first motion picture in 1894: during the next eighteen years, it amassed over 5,000 films in the form of paper prints, many of which have since been rephotographed and restored for viewing. The Museum of Modern Art began acquiring prints of significant features and shorts in 1935, with an eye to building a comprehensive survey of important world cinema. The film collection of the International Museum of Photography at George Eastman House was initiated in 1948 and holds many rare, original prints and negatives. These institutions were joined in their archival efforts in recent years by the American Film Institute and the UCLA Film, Television, and Radio Archives.

Preservation is not a simple process, but one which involves at least four aspects:

First, endangered films must be located and acquired. Early films have been donated by corporations and by thousands of individuals: they have been recovered from expected sources, such as studio and laboratory vaults, as well as from the unlikeliest locations, such as basements and garbage dumps. Archival acquisition also means that pertinent copyright laws and donor restrictions must be observed at all times.

Second, films must be catalogued. Information about the film's production and cast must be gathered in accordance with established cataloguing guidelines. Film fragments, of course, present problems for archivists and cataloguers.

Third, films must be physically preserved and maintained. Nothing can be done to stop the eventual deterioration of nitrate-based film stock, although careful storage in temperature- and humidity-controlled vaults tends to slow this process. The primary method of preservation, then, involves transferring films from nitrate materials to acetate, safety stock. In some cases, it is simply a matter of transferring a good nitrate print to a more permanent acetate negative; often, however, the original materials require repair or painstaking restoration work before preservation masters and reference prints can be struck.

Finally, these films must be made available for viewing by the scholarly community in on-site study facilities, and by the populace through public screenings. Touring film exhibitions such as *Before Hollywood* are especially important, as they provide great numbers of people throughout the country with the chance to view and appreciate archival cinema.

In 1984 the National Endowment for the Arts and the American Film Institute established the National Center for Film and Video Preservation to coordinate and implement moving image preservation activities on a national scale. Among the projects initiated by the center is a National Moving Image Database, which will centralize holdings information from the nation's film and television archives. As film archives across the country work together to avoid duplication of effort, they also face a common problem—the lack of adequate funding. The bulk of film preservation funds have been provided by the National Endowment for the Arts. Other foundations, organizations, and agencies have provided valuable support, but more is needed if our film heritage is to be saved for future generations.

Stephen Gong

Offscreen Spaces: Images of Early Cinema Production and Exhibition

by Richard Koszarski

The history of the American cinema is documented not just in writings, but also in images from the period. Long before studio publicity departments began issuing posed views of directors and stars at work on shooting stages and moviegoers enjoying their products, photographers—both amateur and commercial—were, in a more spontaneous way, capturing the activities of pioneer filmmakers and nickelodeon audiences.

Almost a century later, we find our interest shifting from the original subject of these innocent, snapshot-like pictures to what was once considered peripheral to them: decorations on the wall, an arrangement of apparatus, casual visitors loafing at the edge of the frame. Relatively few motion pictures from the first two decades of the cinema have survived, and the culture that produced them has changed utterly. The photographs that follow offer a unique context for understanding the turn-of-the-century films featured in this exhibition.

Hand-drawn posters at the Star Theatre, location unknown, advertise *The Piker's Dream*, a 1907 Vitagraph film, along with two actualities and an illustrated song.

AMERICAN MUTOSCOPE & BIOGRAPH CO. 841 BROADWAY, N.Y.
American Mutosope & Biograph Co. 841 BROADWAY, NEW YORK.
AMERICAN MUTOSCOPE & BIOGRAPH CO. 841 BROADWAY, N.Y.

D. W. Griffith directs Henry B. Walthall in *Death's Marathon*, filmed in April 1913 at Biograph's Los Angeles studio. Billy Bitzer operates a Pathé studio camera, the most widely used camera of the period.

J. Searle Dawley (*center*) directs an unidentified Civil War subject at the Bronx Edison studio, around 1911.

Opposite: The American Mutoscope and Biograph Company sends four cameras to cover the Jeffries-Sharkey fight at the Coney Island Club House, New York, November 1899.

Peter Bacigalupi's Phonograph and Kinetoscope parlor in San Francisco displayed Edison "film posters" on the wall as early as 1894. Before the introduction of a mechanical coin-slot device, each machine was started manually by an attendant.

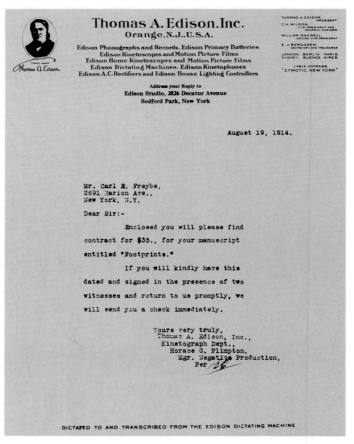

By the end of the nickelodeon era, production at the Edison studio was highly organized, but stories were still purchased over the counter from freelance writers.

Opposite: Fred Ott, an employee at the West Orange Edison studio, performs his specialty in *Edison Kinetoscopic Record of a Sneeze, Jan. 7, 1894*, the first copyrighted motion picture subject.

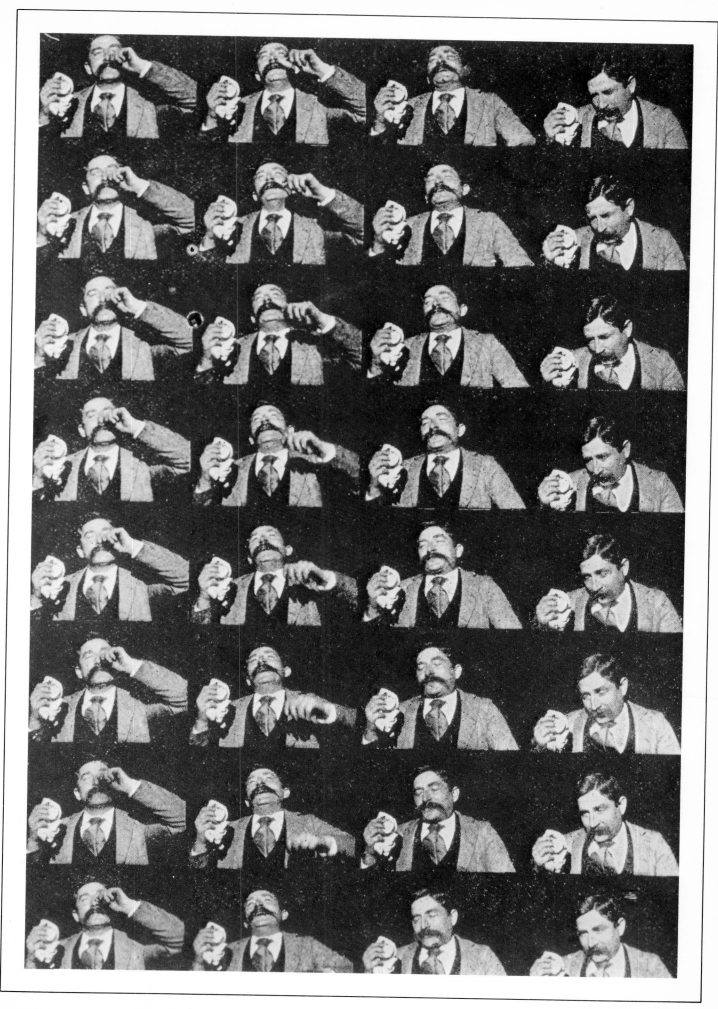

Billy Bitzer takes the Biograph camera to Boston in 1898, in conjunction with a showing at Keith's Theatre. Local views were often made for out-of-town venues.

Edison camera crew and railroad agents prepare to film *Black Diamond Express* at Wysox, Pennsylvania, 1 December, 1896. James H. White and William Heise are the cameramen.

Inventors George Eastman and Thomas Edison pose on the lawn of Eastman's home in Rochester, New York.

"The Black Maria," the motion picture studio constructed by W. K. L. Dickson at Edison's West Orange, New Jersey, facility in 1892.

By the end of the nickelodeon era, great greenhouse studios such as Sigmund Lubin's in Philadelphia allowed several companies to film simultaneously and boosted sunlight with banks of artificial light.

The brownstone studio and offices of the American Mutoscope and Biograph Company, 11 East 14th Street in Manhattan, as it looked when D. W. Griffith worked there ca. 1909.

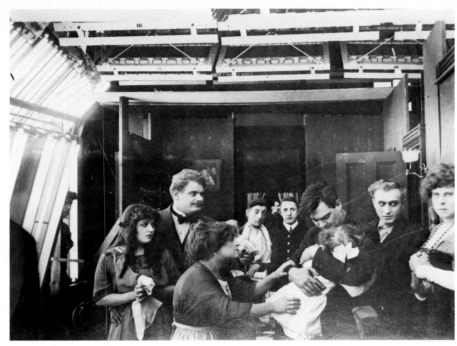

Alan Hale and Lionel Barrymore, two Griffith "discoveries," work on a Klaw and Erlanger feature at the Biograph studio in the Bronx, 1914. Note proximity of studio lights.

Interior of the 14th Street Biograph studio showing banks of Cooper-Hewitt mercury vapor tubes, the most common studio lights of the period.

The 1915 fire that destroyed the Famous Players studio on West 26th Street in Manhattan suggests one reason for the poor survival rate of early motion picture prints.

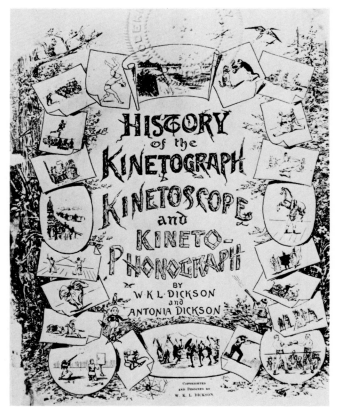

Title page of the first book of film history, issued by W. K. L. Dickson in 1895.

The International Theatre and its staff, Los Angeles, 1910. The exact role of immigrant entrepreneurs as nickelodeon operators remains difficult to assess.

Photoplay, January 1914 and August 1915. The magazine, founded in 1911, played a key role in the promotion of the star system.

Left, cover of program for presentation of *Young Romance* at the Germantown Theatre, Philadelphia, 4 and 5 March, 1915. Right, cover of program brochure of The Strand, a self-described "photo playpalace," December 1915.

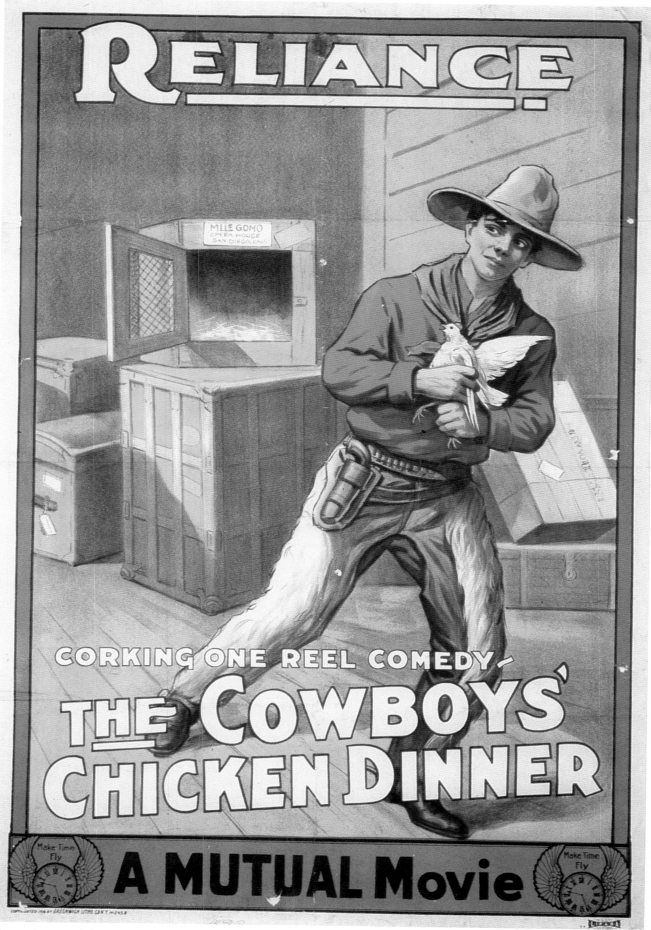

Characteristic stone lithograph motion picture poster of 1914, 27″ × 41″, the standard one-sheet size. Note reference to film's reel length and genre, emphasis on corporate tradenames "Reliance" and "Mutual," and lack of any technical or performer credits.

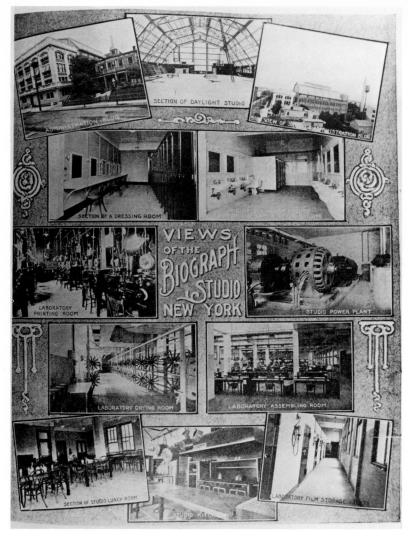

Views of Biograph studio, 807 East 175th Street, Bronx, New York, 1914.

Rooftop studio at Biograph's original location, 841 Broadway, Manhattan, 1897. Stage rotates to face sun.

Views of the Vitagraph studio, at East 15th Street and Locust Avenue, Brooklyn, New York, ca. 1914.

Tom Santschi (at table) working at the Vitagraph studio, ca.1910. Note overhead Aristo Arcs and special double-lens camera for simultaneous production of duplicate original negative.

Edison studio and stock company, Bronx, New York, 1909.

Edwin S. Porter (*left*) directs *A Country Girl's Seminary Life and Experiences*, at the Edison Bronx studio, 1908.

J. Searle Dawley directs at the Edison Bronx studio, 1911. Note electrically driven camera on mobile pedestal, operated by Henry Cronjager, and overhead Aristo Arcs for illumination.

C. J. Williams directs *Amateur Night* at the Edison Bronx studio, 1910.

Poster used by traveling motion picture exhibition company, ca. 1900. As with most cinema posters of this period, the film-viewing experience itself is the topic.

Lantern slide used between reels in small picture houses, ca. 1910–15.

Interior of the Boody Theatre, location unknown, ca. 1910. Note projection port in rear and sparcity of decor in this simple motion picture house.

As early as 1914, film-going had become a popular topic of satire.

The Orpheum Theatre, 1910, location unknown. This legitimate house offered both live acts and film; note orchestra pit and projection booth at rear of balcony.

New Eagle Theatre, Red Granite, Wisconsin, 1911. Films shown here appear to have been accompanied only by piano, although solitary chair at left suggests the presence of additional instruments.

Bill posters relax as moving pictures share a program with illustrated songs, parlor magic, and buck-and-wing dancing (July 1908, location unknown).

Disreputable "store shows" like this one became the inevitable target of censors and pressure groups. A 1914 Thomas Ince melodrama shares the bill with bullfight pictures and sensationalistic footage of Harry K. Thaw, murderer of Stanford White.

Charging ten cents admission, this Onset, Massachussets, theater already boasted of its superior technical equipment.

The use of licensed films from Vitagraph, Kalem, and Selig was heavily emphasized by this 1914 theater.

In 1910 the Electric Theater in East St. Louis, Illinois, felt little need for posters, banners, or other advertising signage.

The Colonial Theatre in Bloomington, Illinois, ca. 1908, used only the brand names of film manufacturers to attract its audience.

By 1915 this theater, location unknown, was not only promoting the titles of individual films, but using a variety of stock poster sizes to do so, including large three-sheet and smaller one-sheet lithographs.

A three-reel program changed three times each week meant that the Arcade Theatre in Los Angeles required nine reels of programming every seven days. Sunday performances were not permitted in all localities.

The baby carriages lined up outside testify to the presence of nursemaids or nonworking mothers in the audience of this urban neighborhood nickelodeon, location unknown.

A traveling company featuring motion pictures and live entertainment stopped in this small Wisconsin town and put up its own portable ticket booth, ca. 1915.

Hollywood in 1905, facing south, before the first filmmakers arrived. Orange Drive runs down the right side of this picture – where it intersects with Hollywood Boulevard, Graumann's Chinese Theatre would later stand. Building in the foreground is now the headquarters of the American Society of Cinematographers; all other structures are gone.

Cellulose Nitrate Roots:
Popular Entertainments and the
Birth of Film Narrative

by John L. Fell

Someday Victorian entertainments such as stereograph cards, dime novels, and slide shows will no longer be isolated as separate "media." Their linkages, along with movies and music halls and rotogravure, will be seen instead as braided strands in the skein of narrative storytelling, information dispensing, and amusement, connecting two centuries of popular culture. From circuses to prime-time television, entertainment has always fed on antecedent materials, and newborn film was no different. The length, structure, and often content of early film evolved from other forms of popular entertainment.

Delegated to find subjects for the 50-foot loops that ran through the Edison Company's peep-show kinetoscopes, W. K. L. Dickson turned to New York music halls, burlesque, traveling shows, and vaudeville to supply bits of self-contained performance. Each subject had only to be autonomous enough to support its tiny, animated fragment: Annie

Oakley taking potshots at clay targets, Sandow flexing his deltoids, "Madam Rita" dancing, Indians from Buffalo Bill's Wild West Show, which had just closed in Brooklyn, re-enacting a War Council and a Ghost Dance. Dickson also culled five "subjects" from *A Milk White Flag*, one of Broadway's musicals.

In the same vein, documentary footage of such events as the Galveston disaster and the Spanish-American War maintained a single-shot/single-event design, although newsworthiness warranted several productions on a given subject. "Real" and "staged" occurrences merged on occasion; in September 1894 at Edison's New Jersey studio an enlarged kinematographic camera accommodated successive rounds of a match between Pete Courtney, heavyweight boxer from Trenton, and Gentleman Jim Corbett. The

Vaudeville humor in *An Unexpected Knockout* (1901).

39

Searching Ruins on Broadway, Galveston, for Dead Bodies (1900).

Edison film of championship boxing match.

tion raged through the 1890s and into a new century's first decade, staged as often as not among the Sunday features. As movies grew in length and shot-to-shot complexity, the comics progressed from "one-shot" graphics, such as editorial cartoons, to multipanel successions of imagery, their stories ballasted with ballooned dialogue, their lengths measured by the limitations of an unfolded newspaper page.

In Sunday editions full-page color comics ran nine to twelve panels, as they do today. Some successive drawings encapsulated action as it progressed within an unchanging perspective, maintaining one camera angle as it were. To continue the story, other drawings either shifted perspective on the same scene or moved to quite different locations. Thus, in movie parlance, shots might be as many as nine, but more often numbered five or six.

Picture to picture, the likenesses of comic pages to movie

Sunday page of "Captain and the Kids" color comics.

rounds ran 1:16 (minutes:seconds), 1:24, 1:12, 1:29, 1:23, and 0:50.

Perhaps the element of succession—separate events, sequentially viewed—unobtrusively emerged here; fight fans edged from one kinetoscope to another to follow the action. Soon, even greater film capacities were able to stretch out the resources of one continuous camera run, with incidents following each other uninterrupted. *What Happened on Twenty-Third Street* (Edison, 1901) runs 93 feet, and *A Visit to the Spiritualist* (Vitagraph, 1899) measures 100 feet.

Soon after their 1896 premiere at Koster & Bial's, the movies rapidly outgrew kinetoscopes and kinetoscope parlors. Longer projector time could also support productions made of successive scenes. By 1903, several-shot films were unremarkable. If longer than most, the eleven-minute *Great Train Robbery* (Edison, 1903) was hardly uncommon.

Successive-shot movie stories turned to other entertainments in search of narrative patterns, as they did for subject matter. A recurrent "inspiration" was the comic strip. This popular, turn-of-the-century sibling was parented, like movies, by industrial technology, mass distribution, and commercial appeals to semiliterate audiences. Joseph Pulitzer, a Hungarian immigrant, produced the *New York World's* first color page on 9 April 1893. Between the *World* and William Randolph Hearst's *Morning Journal*, competi-

continuity are inescapable. The panel-to-panel "cuts" in the comic strip characteristically maintain screen positions, match action, and direct visual attention with sophistication often well in advance of their film contemporaries. In *Terrible Ted* (Biograph, 1907) the central character wakes from his dream like one of Winsor McCay's restless sleepers in "The Dream of the Rarebit Fiend," a comic strip series later adapted to the screen by Edwin S. Porter.

Several full-page features, such as "The Katzenjammer Kids," "Buster Brown," and "Little Nemo," were headed by page-wide drawings that furnished a kind of topical introduction rather than starting up the day's story immediately. In this function and also because of its typically close-up perspective, the first image reverberated among period films. *The Hundred-to-One Shot* (Vitagraph, 1906), for example, commences with a close-up of a hand clutching large-currency bills, then proceeds to its actual story. *The Fire Bug* (Biograph, 1905) introduces its villain at the film's opening with a medium close-up of the villain holding a torch spotted against a white background and independent of story. With its famous introductory scene of an outlaw firing toward the camera, Edwin S. Porter's *The Great Train Robbery* conforms to the same design.

Comics also supplied story lines and characters to a first generation of film directors. Certainly mischievous boys are not limited to time or place, but they abounded in the early comics. "Buster Brown," "Little Jimmy," and "The Katzen-

Winsor McCay's comic strip, "The Dream of a Rarebit Fiend" (1905).

Edwin S. Porter's film, *The Dream of a Rarebit Fiend* (1906).

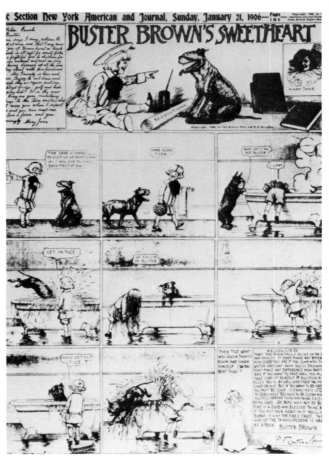

Sunday page of "Buster Brown" comics with "theme" top panel.

jammer Kids" (along with a rival version called "The Captain and the Kids"), painted week-to-week brawling families in which children outwitted parents and were then brought up short, often with a last-panel spanking. Their movie equivalents were legion, starting perhaps with *A Wringing Good Joke* (Edison, 1899). One variation was the Foxy Grandpa series—for example, *The Boys Think They Have One On Foxy Grandpa, But He Fools Them* (Biograph, 1902)—again based on a comic strip. Its author was Charles Schultze who signed his work "Bunny" and in 1900 invented the elderly trickster who slyly outmaneuvered his grandchildren.

Personal (1904).

Meet Me at the Fountain (1904).

Another variant was the battling married couple, with or without children and mother-in-law. Before settling into "Bringing Up Father" in 1913, cartoonist George McManus experimented with "Snoozer," "Alma and Oliver," "The Merry Marcelene," and "The Newlyweds," who soon became "The Newlyweds and Their Baby." Movies supplied many versions of marital spats; errant husbands appeared as regularly in film scripts as they did among stereograph card sets, postcards, and burlesque skits.

In 1904, Biograph initiated a copyright infringement suit against Edison, based on Porter's obvious plagiarism of a

1904 Biograph comedy, *Personal*. Edison's product was *How a French Nobleman Got a Wife Through the New York Herald "Personal" Column* (1904). (Another version, *Meet Me at the Fountain* [Lubin, 1904], escaped legal scrutiny.) Significantly, Porter claimed in defense that Wallace McCutcheon of Biograph had found the story in a comic strip. Untrue this time, it could easily have happened. Few early filmmakers had much, if any, background in the arts. They snatched ideas wherever ideas flourished, and comic pages provided a treasure-trove of proletarian images rendered comfortable. Tramps, old eccentrics, bickering couples, and naughty children, all made the exigencies of turn-of-the-century

W.C. Fields in tramp juggler costume.

Burglar on the Roof (1898).

"Weary Willie and Tired Tim" comic strip.

Americana seem safe and silly.

Tramps, in fact, were common figures in circus and stage comedy, sometimes threatening to family life, but usually harmless or easily cowed by authority. Lew Bloom was a famous bum. W. C. Fields worked several years as a stage vagrant after pilfering the act of a comic named Harrigan, who, like Fields, called himself the tramp juggler. Filmmaker J. Stuart Blackton's movie vagabond probably appeared first in *Burglar on the Roof* (Vitagraph, 1898). The Blackton-Edison *Happy Hooligan* series (seven were on sale in 1900) stemmed from a comic-strip creation by Frederick Burr Opper, hired by Hearst in 1899. Weary Willie, as in *Weary Willie and the Gardener* (Edison, 1901), came from an 1896 strip, "Weary Willie and Tired Tim," drawn by Tom Brown for a British children's magazine, *Illustrated Chips*. The gardener movie was also a steal from another film about a mischievous boy, Lumière's *L'Arroseur arrosé* (1895), and was probably shot by Porter, who made several tramp films that year.

Early movie character types are also easily found in other period entertainments. Some connections link film with the early phonograph, which holds additional interest because, like the player piano, it was the first machinery to invade the American living room. Like the kinetoscopes, cylinders were first merchandised by Edison for coin-in-slot arcades (and for dictation), but by 1899, he was selling a Gem Phonograph for the home, priced as low as $7.50. The unfortunately racist movie *Laughing Ben* (Biograph, 1902) had an equally unfortunate counterpart in "Laughing Coon" (George W. Johnson on Edison cylinder no. 4005). Edison tie-ins were common. The company made two films based on their twenty Casey recordings; *Casey and His Neighbor's Goat* (Edison, 1903) was one. They also made three Uncle Josh movies, such as *Uncle Josh in a Spooky Hotel* (1900); there were forty-four Uncle Josh humorous monologues on Edison cylinders. The recorders and films characteristically made fun of country rubes in the city.

Theater's connections to movies are as old as Dickson's first kinetoscopes, but the relationship is also sturdier and longer lasting than most other forms. Early on, the convention of the *vision scene*, in which a character's mental preoccupation appeared in an upper corner of the screen, was a staple of nineteenth-century melodrama. Deep in traditions of genre, Hawkshaw the detective was a stalwart hero in Tom Taylor's play, *The Ticket of Leave Men* (1863), and had become a comic butt by the time of *Getting Evidence* (Edison, 1906). Vestiges of trained and bravely disposed nineteenth-century stage animals found their way into such film creations as the dog who unties the heroine's bonds in *The Train Wreckers* (Edison, 1905). As the years passed, early silent films have become a kind of visual museum of the stage gestures, sets, and story conventions that were fast disappearing in the wake of Charles Frohman's and David Belasco's movements toward realism on the New York stage.

The years 1906 to 1908 were a kind of rest period, as if the movies had paused momentarily to catch their breath and review their storytelling strategies. Stabilized at a reel's running time (10–12 minutes), most films of this time fell back on a few organizing formulas. The challenge seemed to be to block out a containing form (a dream, for example)

that energized someone and impelled sufficient action to join shots without bewildering the viewer. Chases were so frequent that they exhausted the form more drastically than the pursued and their pursuers. Another recurring pattern was the *motivated link* by which a protagonist was peculiarly distinguished so that his singularity connected a series of otherwise unrelated episodes. In *The Love Microbe* (Biograph, 1907), for example, a scientist injects fighting couples with a serum that produces unexpected affection. The pace of ordinary life is accelerated by electricity in *Liquid Electricity* (Vitagraph, 1907).

Such stories were Sunday comic designs, but in the moment of narrative plateau, they seem prepared to withdraw for the sake of greater plot density. To provide patterns complicated enough to sustain a reel's worth of unflagging entertainment, filmmakers turned more often to

Vision scene in *The Miller's Daughter* (1906).

stage and fiction narrative, building on a broader repository of popular taste and comprehension. One precedent, curiously parallel, was the New York vaudeville season of 1895–96, which introduced little playlets among its billings. Many were tailormade for star performers. Others appeared as suspense stories and melodramas, either cut down from longer material (such as *The Old Homestead*) or original works by such writers as Richard Harding Davis.

Yet where stage playlets simplified and condensed their material, the movies expanded it into interweaving story lines. More *happened* in a post-1908 film by D. W. Griffith or his contemporaries than in many stage playlets of equal length. More happened and *seemed* to happen, because greater attention was paid to events, which stretched out to accommodate the scrutiny.

Under these circumstances, the movies sometimes appeared to be pull against constraints of audience comprehension. The tension created by their efforts to establish variation within the prescribed forms prompted early filmmakers to seek better storytelling methods so that spectators would more clearly understand narratives as they unfolded on the screen.

The means were not unique; they were simply redeployed. As in 1890s fiction and even narrative poems, relatively simple plots were conveyed by complex, nonlinear techniques. In *The Lost Child* (Biograph, 1904), the image of an infant is inserted into a sequence of shots of a mob returning to town after chasing an apparent kidnapper. More thrillingly, in *The Hundred-to-One Shot* exposition is organized so that scenes of a rescuer, driving at breakneck speed to forestall an imminent mortgage foreclosure, are interrupted by a shot of the endangered family. Through such sequencing of shots, relationships between two story strands submitted to narrative manipulation. However common to literature, to Charles Dickens, Frank Norris, or the dime novelists, such narrative strategy was new in the movies. It later became the norm in Griffith's Biograph films of 1909 through 1911.

As the new century wound up its first decade, movie theaters proliferated nationwide. In Boston, for example 84 percent of the auditorium seating capacity (for entertainment) was in its movie theaters by 1909. Film viewing, however, was not limited to the major cities; it spread easily into small town America.

So broad an audience required regular installments of this new product, the motion picture, increasingly formularized now and increasingly fiction as distinguished from documentary. Movie stories drew regularly from middle-class libraries to satisfy the audience's desire for "family entertainment." *Francesca da Rimini: or The Two Brothers* (Vitagraph, 1907) is a fragment out of Dante, and *"Teddy" Bears* (Edison, 1907) combines Goldilocks's adventures with a touch of Teddy Roosevelt's hunting exploits.

Griffith's Biograph sources included comedy, melodrama, and works by writers such as Robert Browning, O. Henry, Bret Harte, and Jack London. While such borrowings suggest a new seriousness on the part of filmmakers, more importantly, they demonstrate equal commitments to a wider variety of story forms and idioms of popular culture. Translated to film in its early years, comics and music-hall turns had appealed to one layer of urban sensibility: people who read the *Morning Journal* and frequented Tony Pastor's or Proctor's 23rd Street Music Hall. The vast new movie audiences were increasingly middle class and family centered.

Griffith's mammoth output, much of it still available, reveals a mind at work, often at rework. For instance, *The Long Road* (Biograph, 1911) can be viewed as an early, somewhat haywire version of the feature *True Heart Susie* (Paramount-Artcraft, 1919). Pressured by Biograph to make melodramas and adhere to production schedules, Griffith turned inward to Griffith more often than to Dickens. *A Girl and Her Trust* (Biograph, 1912) is a literal remake of *The Lonedale Operator* (Biograph, 1911), and *An Outcast Among Outcasts* (Biograph, 1912) is yet another variation of the identical plot.

In such stories besieged women were predictably rescued. Violence is as American as John Philip Sousa, and Griffith's melodramatic plots (in which gypsies, bums, Indians, blacks, and biblical tyrants were often interchangeable heavies) enlisted audience enthusiasms by whetting interest in how rescues were to be effected and to be shown. It is in the minutiae of threat, suspense, and brave invention that Griffith impresses with his developing arsenal of technique. Measuring no longer than his early films, the later Griffith Biographs contain many more shots, movements, and premeditated stagings than those of 1908 and 1909. With his protagonists regularly faced with death or worse, the director concentrated on the voltages powering anxious audience excitement, the electrical circuitry of melodrama's old Victorian mansion.

The romance novel in *Maiden and Men* (1912).

To a broad base of middle-class sensibility, the Janus face of American violence was gentility. Certainly many younger members among the growing movie audiences were romantically disposed, and some period films offered amusing insights into popular fantasy. At least three movies in the *Before Hollywood* exhibition share a single theme: their protagonists read from the printed page. In *Terrible Ted*, the book is a dime novel and the reader, a boy, dreams of adventure in the Wild West. In *Maiden and Men* (American Film Manufacturing, 1912), the book is a romance entitled *Her Secret Treasure*; infused with its fantasy, a girl descends from the hills to a valley ranch where life contradicts her vision. In *Young Romance* (Lasky, 1919), the boy and girl are both fans of romantic pulp adventure and share a real experience livelier than the printed page.

In each case, the story within the written text reflected the film's own story. The sensibility of one was inscribed on the other; the story was about itself, and from the first film to the third, it turned progressively genteel. It also took progressively longer to tell. *Terrible Ted* runs one reel in length; *Maiden and Men* is three reels; and *Young Romance* is a five-reel "feature" length. The developing sensibility was also reflected in the films' own expositions. As relationships became more delicately phrased, an older stage repertory of conventional gesture and facial mime lost its capacity to reflect appropriate states of mind. For an actor or actress to affect and react to the "action" required increasingly subtle and even self-contradictory emotional responses, just as the actions were themselves far more nuanced. "Feelings" required wider ranges of performance, which in turn depended increasingly on visual intimacies. Actors played to the camera rather than to an imagined audience behind the camera.

In the process, moral polarities sometimes became blunted or obscured. For example, in *Indian Massacre* (Ince, 1912), an out-and-out melodrama, an Indian woman and a woman settler share a common grief at their material losses, and plot symmetries suggest some kind of ethical reciprocity. In earlier films, villains acted out little more than a checklist of threats to couples and families (by kidnapping, theft, seduction, foreclosure, infidelity). In the next series of films, fed by shifts in popular literature, by the rise of new, popular magazines, and by such influences as Belasco's theater, values appeared to be less sharply defined. As American film approached World War I, it seemed almost to anticipate a growing confusion over right and wrong.

A Subversive Form

by Neil Harris

Writing for the *Atlantic Monthly* in the summer of 1900, the novelist Rupert Hughes mused on a recent spate of what he called "accidental" or "chance" literature. An older version consisted on the "fortuitous charm of dictionaries, directories, concordances, gazetteers,"[1] impressive assemblies of extraordinary information, but a new and powerful form had emerged in places like New York. This was the "belles lettres is signboards, romances set up so that he who runs may read, and stop running."[2] Immigration and economic growth had brought a remarkable set of names affixed to prominent signs to American cities. Attached to storefronts, advertising boards, and railings, these announcements were invariably unsigned. Their words and pictures were designed to encourage patronage. The imaginative pedestrian could construct fantastic sequences based on the arbitrary linkage of names from signboards. The results, Hughes believed, would challenge the novels of Alexandre Dumas for exotic fascination.

Defining this unusual genre, Hughes unwittingly touched on one of the many links tying the infant motion pictures to the larger culture of the day and on one of the factors that had prepared film audiences for the special nature of the movies. By 1900 most traditional art forms had developed clear protocols for authorship. Whether visual or literary, works of art were signed in some way so that clients, critics, readers, and viewers could pursue their favorites. Orders of reputation and precedence were established based on some knowledge of authorship. Schools, occupational history, exhibitions, competitions, commissions, and publishers supplied effective pedigrees for the successful competitors.

By the 1890s, image making had undergone a revolution which challenged the certifying power of individual reputation. Changes in printing technology and distribution had stimulated a vast array of designs created by hands as anonymous as those that built the medieval cathedrals or produced the cave paintings at Lascaux. Advertising illustrations, labels, wrappers, postcards, book covers, title pages, logos, trademarks, billboards, all were designed by individual artists, but unlike traditional literary and visual

Reenacting a widely publicized kidnapping in *The Black Hand* (1906).

Watching a (Biograph) movie in *The Story the Biograph Told* (1904).

artworks, very few were signed. Some authors and designers left clues to their identity or established coherent styles whereby historical investigation can reconstruct some personal achievements, but much remains unknown. The anonymity of these images, their many duplications, their collective (or corporate) auspices, and their variations on easily recognized motifs summed up several conventions of modern mass production. Although the artistic merit of these designs was secondary to their informational value, the pictures and phrases exerted a powerful influence on popular consciousness. They expressed what promoters believed the public would find appealing, interesting, or moving.

In the early days, motion pictures also exposed enormous audiences to just this kind of anonymous presentation. While the copyrighted emblem, so coyly presented in individual frames, announced the production company, we know little about who made decisions concerning subject, story, sequence, or camera shot. Credits are brief; even performers go unmentioned. Such anonymity bestows on these films some of the problems confronting archaeologists as they unearth shards of an ancient culture. The first age of film occurred less than a century ago, but these early movies possess a primitive, almost hieratic quality, a touch of mystery which can hush the most irreverent audience. It is not caused by the antiquity of the message or the wide abyss of time separating the movie makers from curious modern

viewers. It is caused by something else, more difficult to describe.

When new recording technologies first appear, their novel effects threaten conventional notions of time and place. Nineteenth- and twentieth-century Americans and Europeans, self-conscious about their modernity, progressivism, and science, were nonetheless surprised again and again by new miracles of recording light and sound.

Passengers glimpsed during *Interior N.Y. Subway, 14th Street to 42nd Street* (1905).

Getting Evidence (1906).

Meet Me at the Fountain (1904).

These technologies permitted glimpses of things never before seen or heard in just that way—slowed down, speeded up, with expanded volume or diminished scale—a moment preserved beyond its normal duration or cancelled with another equally powerful sound or image. During these first years filmmakers and their public were being initiated into a mystery. Fundamental magic was being created. Rules were not yet clear, and important discoveries seemed to come unexpectedly. Films revealed how the collective organization of very different skills and specialties could produce something that moved beyond the individual imagination.

These very first films make up the first phases of what would eventually become a complex ritual performance. There is a clear suggestion of something being born, as ordinary actions expose their visual logic. Like the first photographs and the first phonograph records, the motion pictures suggest tribal pockets containing awe, wonderment, and delight with a new toy. The odd obsessions and mysterious tastes revealed by the early movies are puzzling until one recalls how obsessive the interest in simple movement must have been.

There is, for example, the startling frequency of the movie chase scene. By 1910 innumerable (and interminable) sequences had been shot of people running after automobiles, animals, other people, or almost anything. *The Lost Child* (Biograph, 1904), *The Greens Good Men* (Vitagraph, 1905), *Jack the Kisser* (Edison, 1907), *The Train Wreckers* (Edison, 1905), *Getting Evidence* (Edison, 1906)—comedies, tragedies, and documentaries—all featured these scenes. "Pursuits of malefactors are by far the most popular of all nickel deliriums," Barton W. Currier wrote in 1907.[3] From Cape Town to Medicine Hat, pursuer and pursued ran for miles, until the prey "collided with a fat woman carrying an umbrella, who promptly sat on them and held them for the puffing constabulary."[4]

Chase scenes belonged partly to older melodramatic conventions that had been transferred to film. By opening up space, motion pictures made it possible to add to the suspense and variety of this kind of dramatic action. Chase scenes also reflected a fascination with the human body in rapid motion. Seeing what happened to human beings as they were propelled through space absorbed both moviemakers and audiences. Early films contained a broad range of human types, at work and play, but never more so

than when a chase was under way. Not only were the participants varied in age and dress, but their very physiognomies were selected for added variety. The unlikely subjects of the camera ranged from fat to skinny to tall to short; there were people on crutches or in wheelchairs, people pushing baby carriages, carrying ladders, wearing elaborate clothing or revealing clothing, leaning on canes, or fettered by leg casts. All of them underwent contortions and distortions that established a graphic record of the body's responses to strain, excitement, and violent action. More than half a century later, audiences are still obsessed by man in motion, but this time the setting is the vast gravityless environment of space where movement produces an eerie mixture of clumsiness and elegance.

As audiences watched the first movies, seeing things that had never been observed before, it was not always necessary for the scenes to be literally authentic. It certainly flattered

Seventy-First Infantry Embarking (1898).

one's sense of self-importance to watch actual troop maneuvers during the Spanish-American War or to view great parades or prizefights involving famous athletes. However, in some of these documentaries, the scenes were reenactments, and the audiences were just as happy with them. The boxing match, real or staged, conveyed body movements with a visual precision undiminished by the fact that actors

G.W. "Billy" Bitzer filming with the Biograph camera (ca. 1898).

Onlookers wave in *The Hold-Up of the Rocky Mountain Express* (1906).

Rube and Mandy at Coney Island (1903).

side of the victims of misfortune rather than that of representatives of the establishment. Crime was sometimes presented sympathetically. Ridicule punctured authority and loaded the very wealthy with satire. The early urban audiences were street-wise. While inclined to be sentimental about personal attachments—romance, children, animals—they were more skeptical of abstract generalizations.

Rural Americans, who for most of the nineteenth century were identified with moral virtue and political independence by poets, politicians, and clergymen, also received ironic treatment. The hick wandering about an exposition midway or falling from one embarrassment into another on a European vacation, hardly advertised the virtues of rural ways, nor did the rube dance and horrible tar-and-feathering of the chicken thief in the aptly named *Fun on the Farm* (Lubin, 1905). In these treatments, country life seemed crude and narrowing.

Moving to the suburbs also failed to achieve that romanticized landscape so beloved in American art and literature. In Biograph's 1904 short *The Suburbanite*, a series of calamities were brought on by a well-meant decision to provide a nicer environment for the children; a drunken cook, incompetent laborers, visiting mother-in-law, missed commuter train, all suggested some of the daily hazards of life outside the city.

Moralists might find this bothersome, but actually these themes were simply variations on old conventions. English playwrights had been working country bumpkins into their comedies for centuries, and metropolitan pleasures or pains had long been celebrated or decried by artists and writers. Sympathy for criminals or victims, and skepticism and irony were also long-established literary modes. The subjects and arguments of films were less subversive than the form itself. In these early days, when filmmakers were so dependent on improvisation and before technical formulas froze their options, films had something of the fragmentary quality of dreams about them. Their discontinuities and strange juxtapositions were more surrealistic than the most avant-garde modernist.

Unlike earlier visual artists, filmmakers did not attempt to create symbols of unity for a fragmenting culture. The heroic statues and allegorical murals, the civic monuments and new urban centers, the stage sets of world's fairs, all

had mimed the specific fight. This interest in watching bodies being subjected to various forces and disciplines may account in part for the continuing production of fight scenes in film and television. The actors are rarely hurt and their acrobatic relationships almost suggest dance.

Story lines in the early films, meandering through genres and categories, were often weak and strained. Individual films were brief and were billed with others so different that any sustained mood was impossible in the theater setting. Audiences were apparently not troubled by the casual production methods or the unconvincing plots. These short dramas were simply excuses for sharing experiences, making observations, and offering judgments. Just as the journalists found it interesting and profitable to record their mental associations while taking trolley rides, cataloguing pedestrians, and observing signs and storefronts, so these short films satisfied taste by making connections between casual actions. The line between authentic footage and reenactments was blurred as easily as the line between documentary and fiction. The integrity of any dramatic category was less crucial than maintaining interest in the visual movements projected on the screen.

It was the concentration on the accidental, arbitrary, and absurd postures human beings assumed that provided much of the really subversive quality of these first films. Moralists were worried about other things. Filmmakers, many of whom came from the working class, were eager to strike a chord in audiences of their peers. Their films often took the

The Suburbanite (1904).

enjoying an autumn renaissance in early twentieth-century America, inhabited another world. The first films had more to do with deception and false identity than with common values or beliefs. Delusion and deception were common, delusion about rural virtue, personal courage, or even physical beauty. Preening, flirting, mockery, and humiliation were abundant. Like the comics in the Sunday newspapers or the vaudeville skits, films subverted because their mode of presentation challenged traditional artistic authority. Hard-working widows, lost children, encircled regiments, and friendless orphans, those traditional props of melodrama, were invoked time and again but with a difference. Caricature was so basic to films, physical distortion so

Grotesques in *Meet Me at the Fountain* (1904).

temptingly easy—as they were to cartoonist and vaudevillian—that the moralizing messages were easily undercut. Film's major impact came through specific details rather than instructive ideals.

In a culture absorbed with consolidating and organizing its heritage and expanding its cultural institutions, the film form was briefly anomalous. In time it too would be polished to a respectable finish, and critics would note approvingly the entry of more sophisticated and complex plots, more accomplished actors, and authoritative directors. Authorship would be as clearly marked as in any of the high arts, and critics would theorize about the fundamental contributions and propensities of this new medium. Rules would distinguish documentary from staged footage, even though they would pose their own problems of definition. But in their first years, films demonstrated that a new kind of art form was possible, combining improvisational genius and convincing illusionism with permanence and portability. The fragmented world of the spectators, speeded up, broken down, intruded on, and laced with haphazardly recorded news and information, had found its own instrument of recreation. And for early film audiences, the museum, library, and schoolhouse would never again be quite the same.

1. Rupert Hughes, "Contributors' Club," *Atlantic* 86 (August 1900), pp. 141–42.
2. Ibid.
3. Barton W. Currier, "The Nickel Madness," *Harper's Weekly* 51 (24 August 1907), p. 1246.
4. Ibid.

Scene Design and the Early Film

by Brooks McNamara

In 1898 the Eden Musée, a New York City "dime museum," presented a motion picture reenactment of the famous Oberammergau *Passion Play*. Filmed on the roof of Grand Central Station, the *Passion Play* used costumes and probably sets from Salmi Morse's unsuccessful New York stage adaptation of the great Bavarian pageant. Whether the scenery was Morse's or not, the sort of sets common to theatrical productions of the day were employed throughout the film.

The results were generally unimpressive. Painted to be viewed on a gaslit stage, the sets looked crude and stark when filmed by daylight. The overall effect was amateurish and anachronistic—especially since the film also contained footage actually made in the town of Oberammergau. The contrast between the obvious theatricality of some scenes and the reality of others appears inconsistent to us today. But at the turn of the century, there apparently seemed to be nothing especially odd about such a juxtaposition. As a matter of course, American films of the day used a hodge-podge of scenic backgrounds. Some of them clearly borrowed traditional theater sets; others employed actual out-

door locations; many used both. By the teens, however, there had developed a more consistent and integrated approach to the design of the story film, an approach that would continue to influence the look of the American motion picture from that day to this.

Some early filmmakers employed neutral backgrounds for the filming of vaudeville acts and similar small-scale attractions. Others probably improvised sets using the kind of scenic drops that were found in portrait photographers' studios of the period. But theatrical scene design represented a logical solution to the problem of creating suitable backgrounds for multiscene story pictures. Some early studios, in fact, almost certainly used actual stage scenery—acquired second-hand, rented, or purchased new from one of the companies that supplied stock scenery to theaters. Other studios employed carpenters and painters trained in the theater. Thus the theater became a central reference point—probably *the* central reference point for the construction and painting of many sets for the early story film.

Demolishing a set in *Smashing a Jersey Mosquito* (1902).

The Passion Play of Oberammergau (1898).

Documentary footage of the town of Oberammergau (1900).

Annabelle Serpentine Dance (1895).

Filming *Annabelle Serpentine Dance* (1895).

Scenic drops in turn-of-the-century portrait photographer's studio.

(In a notable 1903 borrowing from the theater, Edwin S. Porter transferred to the screen not only the sets, but the costumes, lighting effects, and actors from one of several companies touring New Jersey in *Uncle Tom's Cabin* at the time.)

The conventions of theatrical scenery at the turn of the nineteenth century were quite different from those of today. Realistically detailed sets, which created the illusion of actual places, were being used in a limited way at the time. But most Americans who attended the theater were presented with thoroughly traditional stock sets—often the same sort of painted side wings and drops that had been in common use since the eighteenth century and made no attempt to represent particular locations except in the most off-hand way. In the main, theatergoers still accepted such scenery as a perfectly logical and appropriate stage convention.

Harlowe Hoyt, whose family ran a theater in Beaver Dam, Wisconsin, in the 1880s and 1890s, recalled that besides "the front drop, the house scenery consisted of two curtains with side flats to match. One curtain was an elaborate parlor with a prison interior on its reverse. The other was a kitchen or a bosky wood, depending upon the side displayed. So, too, with the flats. A prison wall could become a tree and a parlor 'pillar and urn' a dingy kitchen wall."[1]

Such conventionalized utility scenery was found everywhere. A traveling tent show in the first years of the twentieth century often carried only four basic sets, called *front room*, *back room*, *timber*, and *town*. As showman Neil Schaffner recalled, "The *town* set consisted mainly of a drop showing a street scene; *timber* was a woodland setting, and *back room* was a plain chamber that usually served for a kitchen set. *Front room* really was two sets. One represented a parlor in an ordinary home and the other, known as a *center door fancy*, represented a rich man's drawing room. The fancy had an arch up center, a door right and a door left and it practically always contained a table and two chairs right and a settee left. Some radical directors changed things around and put the table and chairs left and the settee right, and some even went so far as to put the settee center, flanked by the armchairs."[2]

Much of this sort of stock scenery was purchased from commercial scene painters' catalogues. A considerable amount of it was probably fairly well done, as far as it went, although typically three-dimensional detail was merely painted on a drop or flat and did not bear very close inspection. The best of such scenery, however, was certainly effective on the rather dimly lit stages still found in many theaters, where kerosene footlights or overhead gas fixtures provided relatively soft illumination.

Such was not the case when the films employed sets designed in the theatrical scenic tradition. Harsh daylight was necessary for filming, and cinema's early scene designers seem not to have fathomed—or not to have cared—that they were working in a new medium. Their products look strident: architectural molding is not three-dimensional; the canvas on flats flaps in the breeze; the flats themselves are crudely joined; interiors often seem to bear only the most tangential relationship to the action going on inside them; and exterior settings, with their obviously painted foliage, are especially ineffective.

Victorian scene painter's catalogue illustration.

Daylight filming at Sigmund Lubin's rooftop Philadelphia studio (ca. 1899).

The early film designers, however, seem to have solved the problem of the exterior set in a new if somewhat inconsistent way. Gradually, while continuing to use stock interior sets designed in the theatrical manner, they began to take advantage of an option not given to theater designers—they began to film their exterior scenes in actual outdoor locations. In doing so they created an odd disunity from scene to scene in their pictures: the characters in their films moved between obviously *real* places and patently theatrical, *unreal* places. Yet, the introduction of the "location" as a background for action was a perfectly logical outgrowth of the possibilities inherent in the new film medium.

Among the earliest films were the *actualities*, little slices of real life transferred to the motion picture screen. Thousands of these films were turned out during the first several years of motion picture production. Whether it was a burning building, a speeding freight train, tourists promenading at Coney Island, or soldiers debarking from a troop ship during the Spanish-American War, the spectator saw actual events happening in an actual place. Usually the place was outdoors, since ample natural light was necessary to the filmmaking process. But the point is that both the event and the place were real. It was only a small step from these actualities to the idea of story films in which fictitious events

Lighting equipment used for Biograph Company subway films (ca. 1905).

Interior N.Y. Subway, 14th Street to 42nd Street (1905).

were shown in real places. An important difference, however, lay in the fact that, in these story films, locations were selected not merely becase they were real, but because they represented plausible backgrounds for the purely fictitious events being filmed.

In a film called *Rube and Mandy at Coney Island* (Edison, 1903), for exmple, Steeple Chase, one of the famous Coney Island amusement parks, serves as background for the adventures of a pair of country bumpkins. Unlike the actualities, the emphasis is not on the park and its conventional activities. Instead, the film centers around a fictitious couple and their tour of Steeple Chase, which becomes, in effect, a set. The difference between it and a conventional stage set is merely that it was selected instead of being constructed and painted. But the result is that the real Steeple Chase looks very different from the sort of traditional stage scenery that was used in other films. It is not a

stock scenic representation of a place, but a genuinely real place of the sort that came to provide a laboratory for change in film composition and acting style. Film directors, temporarily freed from the restrictions of the stage set in such outdoor scenes, could use their cameras with greater flexibility. Film actors, responding to the same freedom, could experiment outdoors with approaches to movement and gesture that would have been inconceivable onstage. But as yet there was little consistency to their experiments or to the concept of film design.

In *Rube and Mandy at Coney Island*, as in many other story films of the day, a real place is seen in juxtaposition with a totally different design convention. At one point in the film, Rube and Mandy are shown eating hot dogs before a completely neutral background. Perhaps most often in films of this period, real exterior locations alternated with obviously stock interior sets. In *The Suburbanite* (Biograph,

Rube and Mandy at Coney Island (1903).

The Suburbanite (1904).

The Suburbanite (1904).

The Miller's Daughter (1905).

The Miller's Daughter (1905).

1904), for example, real outdoor scenes alternate with an obviously painted dining-room set and a kitchen set in which a shelf of pots and pans is actually painted on the flats in the most conventional theatrical manner. But any combination was possible, and in *The Miller's Daughter* (Edison, 1905) actual shots of the Flatiron Building were featured along with a stagy exterior set of a waterfall.

Until about 1910, this curious approach to design seems to have been more or less standard practice with filmmakers. Gradually, however, an important change was taking place in their scenic practice; the conventionalized interior set was being brought into line with the exterior location. That is, interiors were beginning to be constructed and painted so that they appeared to be actual rooms in the real buildings—not stage sets. Thus films began increasingly to present a unified design scheme. The reasons for the shift are not altogether clear. In part, it probably took place simply because film design, like the medium itself, was beginning to achieve some maturity and sophistication. The design of film sets was becoming a specialty in its own right, and thus more attention was being paid to a coherent and integrated use of the set as one of many elements in a film.

An improved technology and a new emphasis on design research helped to make the shift possible. Lighting equipment and construction techniques were less primitive, and for the first time some concerted effort was made to research decorative details and to dress sets properly. Ear-

lier sets had usually been dressed with an *ad hoc* collection of properties. By 1910, however, there is a clear interest in enhancing a film's environment through the use of props that make sense in terms of time and place and story being told. In a Civil War melodrama, *The Informer* (Biograph, 1912), for example, there is an obvious attempt to create period authenticity both through the architectural detail of the set and through appropriate properties.

There is almost certainly another influence on film

The Informer (1912).

David Belasco's 1901 production of *The Auctioneer*.

C.B. DeMille's film version of Belasco's *The Girl of the Golden West* (1915).

design, as well—which returns us once again to the theater. The film industry's move toward the creation of detailed realistic interiors was not simply an attempt to bring them into line with the real exteriors that were being used. Another obvious influence was the popular realism of Broadway producer-director David Belasco and his imitators in the theater. If much of the turn-of-the-century tradition of theatrical set design was generalized and conventional, there was a developing interest in the novel concept of detailed realism on stage.

The concept reached its zenith in Belasco's productions of such plays as *The Easiest Way* (1909), in which he transferred a genuine boarding house bedroom to the stage; *The Girl of the Golden West* (1915), which contained meticulously naturalistic barroom scenes; and the famous *Governor's Lady* (1912), which featured an accurate re-creation of a Childs Restaurant, stocked with food that was actually consumed by the actors onstage. A number of Belasco's immensely popular productions were later filmed with all of the detailed realism that had made Belasco so famous on Broadway.

The novelty of Belasco's intensely realistic settings was not lost on such film directors as Cecil B. DeMille, who reverently noted that "beyond Belasco's realism the stage could hardly go. There the camera was needed."[3] Clearly the controversial New York stage director helped to buttress the move toward realism in film design. By about 1915, such first-class films as *The Cheat* (Lasky) were featuring interiors that were virtually identical to the sort of thing pioneered by Belasco on stage. Increasingly, for good or ill, a kind of seamless realism became the hallmark of American film design, and by the 1920s the old rough-and-ready approach to the set had become a part of American film history.

1. Harlowe R. Hoyt, *Town Hall Tonight* (New York: Bramhall House, 1955), p. 16.
2. Neil E. Schaffner, with Vance Johnson, *The Fabulous Toby and Me* (Englewood Cliffs, N.J.: Prentice-Hall, Inc., 1968), p. 18.
3. Cecil B. DeMille, *The Autobiography of Cecil B. DeMille* (Englewood Cliffs, N.J.: Prentice-Hall, Inc., 1959), p. 19.

The Changing Status of the Actor

by Charles Musser

The Kalem Girl is charming,
And fair as the flowers in May.
Her eyes are the sweetest upon the screen:
They have stolen my heart away.[1]

The year 1915 was one of accomplishment and triumph for the still young film industry. D. W. Griffith's *The Birth of A Nation* was released and quickly hailed as cinema's first masterwork. Poet Vachel Lindsay published *The Art of the Moving Picture*, comparing the movie house to an art gallery, while Harvard philosopher Hugo Munsterberg wrote *The Photoplay: A Psychological Study*, contending that cinema was a major art form of the twentieth century. In less than twenty years, film practice had undergone an astounding series of transformations which made this new recognition possible. The changing role and status of the film actor was one aspect of these transformations.[2]

When projected moving pictures were a novelty, in 1896, an exhibitor's program might follow one scene of Annabelle Moore dancing against a black background with another view of a wave crashing against the shore. These subjects were of equal status: only in later years would the subject of

such "scenics" become the background for the actor's performance. Until at least 1904, production personnel, non-professionals, and stage actors took turns performing for the camera. J. Stuart Blackton and Albert Smith alternated working behind and in front of the camera—with Blackton playing the tramp in *Burglar on the Roof* (Vitagraph, 1898) and Smith acting as magician in *The Vanishing Lady* (Vitagraph, 1898). The woman-on-the-street whose dress is lifted by air from a subway grate in *What Happened on Twenty-Third Street* (Edison, 1901) is on a par with the skilled performer in *Trapeze Disrobing Act* (Edison, 1901).

With the rise of story films in 1903–04, actors became a more important part of film production. *Rube and Mandy at Coney Island* (Edison, 1903) is a transitional film in this

The woman-in-the-street in *What Happened on Twenty-Third Street, New York City* (1901).

Anonymous bystanders in *Railway Station Scene* (1897).

Father misses the commuter train in *The Suburbanite* (1904).

regard. In many scenes, Coney Island served as a backdrop for the performers' comic business, but in others the scenic impulse was still dominant. By the time of *The Suburbanite* (Biograph, 1904), the comic characters had assumed a more central position in the mise-en-scène. As a result, the actor's skills were increasingly called upon to create a rudimentary character. Although motion picture acting thus began to emerge as a more unified practice, the motion picture actor as such did not as yet exist. Theatrical personnel usually worked with production companies only for brief periods of time. Stage actor Will Rising was "in hard luck" when he appeared as the judge in *The Kleptomaniac* (Edison, 1905).[3] When the Edison Company made *Daniel Boone* (1906), producer Edwin S. Porter and stage manager Wallace McCutcheon hired many of their actors from a theatrical troupe presenting the Wild West show *Pioneer Days* at the New York Hippodrome. Porter and McCutcheon had to adapt their schedule to the actors' principal commitment—the show. To complete their cast, the two collaborators also had a casting call for this one film. In this way, film companies treated each film as an individual project and hired actors on a per film basis. Film acting was part-time, occasional work: a way for stage actors to supplement their income. It also was a form of anonymous employment in most circumstances. A film company rarely revealed the names of its cast: high-toned projects were among the few exceptions.

The casual, intermittent relationship between actors and film companies, prevalent before 1907, proved impractical as these companies increased their rate of production to meet the nickelodeon theaters' insatiable demands for one-reel story films. Efficient production required producers to create permanent stock companies of actors. Film acting soon became salaried employment, requiring a full-time commitment. Actress Gene Gauntier, who had enjoyed some prominence in repertory theater, agonized over her decision to stay with the Kalem Company on a long-term basis.[4] When it came down to making a final choice, players were often persuaded by the steady income received from film work. By 1908, there was a growing group of people who had become professional moving picture actors.

The decision to enter the film industry on a permanent basis was a particularly complicated one for actors conscious of the cinema's low status. Prestigious newspapers such as the *Chicago Tribune* asserted that films shown in nickelodeons encouraged wickedness and "not a single thing connected with them had influence for good."[5] In addition, film acting was considered less artistically demanding than stage performance. David Belasco saw cinema as a pale imitation of the theater, a form of entertainment that would soon lose its popularity. With moving pictures "the audience would always be wholly wanting the indescribable bond of sympathy which existed between the actor and his audience."[6] Action, not acting, was considered the keynote of motion pictures, and cinema apparently required neither the character psychology nor the actor's personality that stage performers brought to their work.

Even as critics were dismissing the film actor's profession, changes in film practice were actively reshaping the actor's role. Fiction films were heavily indebted (both directly and indirectly) to other narrative forms such as the novel, short story, and dramatic work. Story construction assumed a clear hierarchy of characters. For example, *Foul Play* (Vitagraph, 1906) focuses on three primary characters: a man who is framed for a crime, the man's wife, and the villain. The film also includes several secondary characters, such as the bank owner, as well as a cast of bit players. Upon such a hierarchy, the motion picture "star system" was to be constructed. Star systems in related practices such as theater and vaudeville, a cultural preoccupation with authorship, and the audience's desire for realistic yet larger-than-life heroes were just some of the added factors that made this development "logical" and even "natural."

From 1907 through 1909, an implicit contradiction existed between the film narratives with their hierarchy of characters and the methods of production which treated every actor the same way—at least all were paid the same amount. Actors were either regular members of a stock company or day players. Yet the stock company system meant that some actors appeared weekly in a studio's offerings. Regular moviegoers soon recognized leading players and nicknamed them "The Vitagraph Girl" (Florence Turner), "The Kalem Girl" (Gene Gauntier), or "The Biograph Girl" (first Florence Lawrence, later Marion Leonard and Mary Pickford).

Changes in representation techniques enhanced those very qualities that were said to be the mark of a successful stage performance. Biograph director D. W. Griffith, in particular, introduced a more restrained, realistic acting style which developed the psychology of his characters. As he and other directors moved their cameras closer to the performers, the actors' personalities came through with increasing strength. By early 1910, one prominent critic asserted that

. . . a competent actor or actress has practically the same chance of coming to the front on the motion picture stage as he or she has on the ordinary stage. That is what they are doing. So it comes about that the personalities of these good people are of growing interest to the public.[7]

Increasingly the spectator was experiencing not only a character and his/her psychology, but the personality of the actor who created that character as well. One need only contrast Lou Delaney's performances in *Foul Play* (Vitagraph, 1906) and *A Tin-Type Romance* (Vitagraph, 1910) to see the changes wrought in the intervening years.

Production companies, trade papers, and exhibitors were flooded with questions about audience favorites—not only their names, but their marital status. During late 1909, when the Edison Company found itself at a commercial disadvantage with films that were not very popular, the company sought to exploit this interest by featuring its principal players in promotional materials.[8] Such practices were not only designed to popularize company performers, but, by emphasizing the actors' experience with prestigious theatrical companies, they increased the prestige of moving pictures in general and Edison subjects in particular. A few months later, Kalem made another breakthrough: they offered exhibitors a lobby display with the names and pictures of its players. Despite the success of this innovation, *Moving Picture World* cautioned, "While the pictures have attained a distinct prominence in the theatrical field and are now regarded as a standard attraction, the people playing the parts in them are very sensitive about having their identity become known. . . . They have an undisguised impression that the step from regular productions to the scenes before the camera is a backwards one."[9]

Leading actors were increasingly treated as stars, at least on a rudimentary level. Competitive bidding for the services of leading players began in December 1909, when Carl Laemmle hired away Biograph Girl Florence Lawrence for his Independent Moving Picture Company (IMP) and announced that she would be known as the IMP girl. That March, St. Louis newspapers suddenly reported the death of Miss Lawrence. Her many admirers were distraught, and Laemmle, who was almost certainly responsible for this misinformation, capitalized on the publicity with a special tour for his very much alive star.[10] The Vitagraph Company responded to this competitive move by holding "A Vitagraph Night for the Vitagraph Girl" in Brooklyn, New York. The patrons in the jammed theater sang choruses of the popular song "The Vitagraph Girl" and demanded an encore so they could sing it again.[11] Such reactions gave the emerging stars new confidence. When Kalem Girl Gene Gauntier was asked if she had given up the stage, she responded,

Why I haven't given it up. There is just as much art in moving picture acting, and more scope for individuality—and certainly fewer who can do it well, besides a greater field. Who

Foul Play (1906).

A Tin-Type Romance (1910).

knows what will be the status of the motion picture actor in ten years? It is on the flood while the theatrical situation, to put it mildly, is uncertain.[12]

Her faith was to be quickly confirmed.

When Florence Lawrence left Biograph for IMP, Mary Pickford soon took her place. A reviewer commented on "the pleasing kittenish playfulness of the little lady that played ingenue parts" at Biograph and predicted that "she has a future if she doesn't permit her head to get swelled."[13] When Lawrence left IMP for the Lubin Company late in 1910, Laemmle lured Pickford away from Biograph by offering a salary of $175 a week. Laemmle, who understood the commercial possibilities of star power better than most of his contemporaries, did not try to promote her as the next IMP girl, but as Mary Pickford. More than a leading player, she was a star in her own right. Many of her IMP films, such as *The Dream* (1911), were star vehicles. The story's principal function was to foreground Pickford's personality, as the actress became the dominant element of the film. In a marketing ploy, Laemmle, after firmly establishing that Pickford was at IMP, stopped associating her with any specific films in his advertisements. Film exchanges were forced to purchase all the IMP films if they were to get all the Pickford films.

The Dream (1911).

Ancient Temples of Egypt (1912).

Between 1908 and 1911, only truly dedicated spectators or "fanatics," followed the careers of leading players. Even for this group, information was hard to gather. In February 1911, however, the *New York Telegraph* added a motion picture section to its Sunday editions, featuring portraits of leading players from all the companies. Vitagraph's J. Stuart Blackton also started the monthly *Motion Picture Story Magazine* which presented film narratives rewritten as short stories and published photographs and brief biographies of the stars. Both publications were designed for spectators rather than for members of the industry.

Increasingly exhibitors were urged to "play up the personality of the player." To aid their efforts, the Edison Company began to advertise the names of leading actors for each of its films—this by July 1911.[14] The projection of slides as a primitive trailer or coming attraction was one approach: "Run a slide that you've a Vitagraph coming with Miss Turner, and then flash Miss Turner's slide. It is more than doubly effective."[15] Soon the business of promotion was too important to leave to the exhibitor who might—or might not—provide his patrons with the desired information. By mid-1912 several companies were using head titles to credit the leading actors. Edison, still struggling with its relatively unpopular films, went even further and introduced each player with a title caption when he or she first appeared on screen.[16] Short subjects, such as *Ancient Temples of Egypt* (Kalem, 1912), which showed the Kalem stock company visiting the Egyptian ruins, were ways to show actors "behind the scenes" and arouse even greater interest in their private lives as well as on-screen performances. Such innovations in promotion enabled the casual moviegoer to identify the players on the screen.

Biograph, in contrast to virtually all the other companies, refused to divulge even the names of its leading performers. This prompted one angry fan to write,

How do you feel when, attending a play on the legitimate stage, the stupid usher forgets to give you a programme? Rather uncomfortable, eh? You feel like giving Mr. Usher a good, swift kick. At present the Biograph Company is playing the role of the stupid usher—ruining their otherwise good photoplays by the stupid narrow-minded policy of "reticence" that they foolishly adhere to.[17]

Film companies faced a terrible dilemma over the best ways to exploit their key actors. On one hand, "the manufacturer cannot be blamed for wanting to preserve the incognito of player and producer, for the instinct of self-preservation is a natural law and the 'star' system invariably creates abuses" such as salary demands. On the other, "the manufacturer can only avail himself of the advantage derived from the exploitation of personality since the situation has run away from him."[18] While Biograph argued that the company, not the individual players, was the guarantee of quality, its director, Griffith, assured the company's continued favor by turning one actor after another into a popular player. These "anonymous stars" were a contradiction in terms, and the Biograph Company lost many players, tired of anonymity, to its competitors. This was a luxury none of its rivals could afford. Biograph was a classic case of uneven development: advances in one area (Griffith's directorial innovations) allowed the company to be unresponsive in others (promotion).

As the star system emerged, it altered the structure of the industry. By 1911–12, a name player was often the most important commercial element, and salaries reflected this shift. They were said to run from $35 to $75 a week for regular players but up to $400 and $500 in the case of stars.[19] Elite actors justified their cost. When the Majestic Company appeared in late 1911, its success was assured because Mary Pickford was joining the organization—leaving behind Laemmle whose $175 a week must have begun to seem paltry. By the second half of 1912, stars were using their enhanced status to start their own production companies. Gene Gauntier and director Sidney Olcott left Kalem to form the Gene Gauntier Feature Players Company, while Helen Gardner left Vitagraph for a similar purpose. These "authors" of leading roles used their position to claim authorship of the overall film.[20]

The emergence of the star system also had an impact on the mode of representation. Close-ups and other compositional strategies, which were largely absent in films of 1908–09, were developed by directors who were not only interested in telling a clear, logical story but in focusing attention on their popular performers. Griffith's *The Old Actor* (Biograph, 1912) is an interesting deviation from this dominant approach. Mary Pickford, who had rejoined Biograph, was the film's obvious star personality, but she was made to play a supporting role. Moreover, when Griffith uses a closer view, he moves in on the old actor, not Pickford. The director isolates a particular moment when the central character, played by W. Christie Miller (himself an old actor), reads Shakespeare.[21] Role and reality converge.

Within a few years, the film industry had produced and pushed to new extremes a star system similar to that in other cultural practices, notably the theater. This, however, did not mean the acceptance of cinema as an art form by "the better classes of the community." When interviewing the newspaper editors who were not only members of these elite classes but helped to shape their opinion, *Moving Picture World* found that "the present status of the motion picture came in for much hostile criticism," although the opinion makers felt "the pictures will do greater and better things in the future."[22] As Clayton Hamilton then observed as he reflected on cinema's cultural status, "the domain of criticism is co-extensive with the domain of art."[23] Until prominent newspapers reviewed films as cultural works instead of citing them as disturbing examples of low culture, the cinema could not be considered a serious art form. Late in 1911, the *New York Tribune* was still complaining about the film industry's excessive depiction of elopements; it was not until late 1915 or early 1916 that leading members of the New York press—the *Herald*, *Tribune*, *World*, and *Times*—finally offered this kind of attention to select films.

One of the developments crucial to film's elevation in status was the appearance of the feature film. It "raised the moving picture to a plane on which it has won the admiration and loyalty of millions of new followers."[24] Many of these early subjects came from Europe. When the Italian-made *Dante's Inferno* was released in the United States during 1911 in five reels (approximately an hour and a half), it was shown at legitimate theaters with ticket prices as high as seventy-five cents.[25] One particularly important group of films starred Sarah Bernhardt: *Camille* (over two reels, Franco American Film Company, advertised in the United States in February 1912), *Queen Elizabeth* (3 reels, Famous Players Film Company, July 1912) and *La Tosca* (Universal Features, October 1912). Adolph Zukor, theatrical producer Daniel Frohman, and Edwin Porter acquired the American rights to *Queen Elizabeth* and with it convinced James O'Neill, James Hackett, and other theater stars to appear in feature-length adaptations of successful plays. As Zukor explained, "When they learned the elaborate manner in which we are going to stage their productions, their attitude changed. They saw that it would be to their advantage, that it would arouse popular interest not only in their productions but in their personalities as well."[26] Unlike the many American players who had defected to the motion picture industry in previous years, these actors were immensely successful in the theater, catering to the cultural tastes of the "better classes." Their acceptance of cinema, even as a means to record their stage performances for posterity, was an important step that was noted in the press. *Prisoner of Zenda* (Famous Players Film Company, 1913) with James Hackett was even reviewed favorably in New York newspapers. As the *World* observed, "The exhibition was unexpectedly successful for it sustained the interest and suspense of the audience to the end."[27]

When asked about the attitude of the most successful stars toward moving pictures, Daniel Frohman responded, "Most of them are trying to figure out how they can become photoplayers with the most possible grace and with the least possible loss of dignity. But they will soon come to it."[28] The formation of the Jesse L. Lasky Feature Film Motion Picture Company in December 1913 offered such an opportunity for many players. Its first film, *The Squaw Man* (February 1914) was based on a well-known stage play, starred the renowned stage actor Dustin Farnum, and was heartily praised in the press. Four months later Lasky acquired the motion picture rights to Belasco's past and future theatrical productions including *The Girl of the Golden West*.[29] The original stage actors were supposed to re-create their roles whenever possible. While this did not always happen, the Lasky company gained access to actors associated with Belasco. In the case of Cecil B. DeMille's film adaptation, *The Girl of the Golden West* (January 1915), the performances were declared to equal those in the original play. After seeing the film, Belasco praised it and another adaptation as "decidedly artistic successes" and acknowledged that the medium could achieve a realism that eluded him on the stage. The "merciless eye" of the camera could

The Old Actor (1912).

The Girl of the Golden West (1915).

be more demanding than the stage in settings and even—although this went unstated—for actors.[30]

Even before *The Birth of A Nation* was released in February 1915, Frohman articulated an increasingly common position. He claimed that theatrical stars making the transition to film "can degrade their art by appearing in silly and inconsequential subjects, but they can assist themselves as well as their art of the theatre by appearing in dignified dramatic productions."[31] Because moving pictures had a much larger audience base, actors could use the cinema to increase the size of their following. Frohman was also implying that the ideal actor was someone who could move back and forth between theater and moving pictures. As 1915 began, film not only rivaled theater as a source of recognition and financial reward, but, it was felt, offered actors a different kind of artistic challenge.

1. *New York Dramatic Mirror* (5 June 1912), p. 26.
2. Aspects of the star system have been described by other film historians, including Richard Dyer, *Stars* (London: British Film Institute, 1979); and Janet Staiger, "Seeing Stars," *Velvet Light Trap* (Summer 1983), pp. 10–14.
3. Richard Outcault to Edwin S. Porter, 3 or 4 March 1904, Porter Affidavit, Edison National Historic Site, Edison, New Jersey.
4. Gene Gauntier, "Blazing the Trail," unpublished manuscript, Museum of Modern Art.
5. *Chicago Tribune*, 10 April 1907 (reprinted in *Moving Picture World* [20 April 1907], p. 101).
6. "Films and the Drama," *Film Index* (5 September 1908), p. 4.
7. "On the Screen," *Moving Picture World* (3 February 1910), p. 167.
8. *Edison Kinetogram* (1 October 1909), p. 13; and ibid. (15 October 1909), p. 13.
9. "Photographs of Moving Picture Actors. A New Method of Lobby Advertising," *Moving Picture World* (15 January 1910), p. 50.
10. "The IMP Leading Lady," *Moving Picture World* (2 April 1910), p. 517.
11. "A Vitagraph Night for the Vitagraph Girl," *Film Index* (23 April 1910), p. 3.
12. "The Kalem Girl," *Film Index* (7 May 1910), p. 3.
13. *New York Dramatic Mirror* (16 April 1910), p. 18.
14. *Moving Picture World* (15 July 1911), p. 58.
15. "Advertising for Exhibitors," *Moving Picture World* (18 October 1911), p. 195.
16. *New York Dramatic Mirror* (29 May 1912), p. 24.
17. *New York Dramatic Mirror* (18 October 1911), p. 28.
18. "Credit Where Credit is Due," *Moving Picture World* (14 October 1911), p. 107.
19. *Motion Picture Story Magazine* (August 1911), p. 144.
20. Michel Foucault, "What is an Author?" in *Language, Counter-memory and Practice* ed. Donald F. Bouchard (Ithaca Cornell Press, 1977); and Robert Arnold, Nicholas P. Humy, and Ana M. Lopez, "Rereading Adaptation: A Farewell to Arms," *Iris* 1, no. 1 (1983), pp. 101–13.
21. Miller was the second oldest actor in the film business in 1913: *Moving Picture World* (12 April 1913), p. 152.
22. *Moving Picture World* (9 December 1911), p. 792.
23. Clay Hamilton in *The Bookman*, quoted in "Sign of the Harvest," *Moving Picture World* (5 August 1911), pp. 272–73.
24. "Achievements of 1911," *Moving Picture World* (13 January 1912), p. 106.
25. *Moving Picture World* (26 August 1911), p. 530.
26. "Achievements of 1911," *Moving Picture World* (13 January 1912), p. 106.
27. "Complete Play in Movies," *New York World* (19 February 1913), p. 7.
28. *Moving Picture World* (26 October 1912), p. 335.
29. "Lasky Gets Belasco Plays," *Moving Picture World* (6 June 1914), p. 1412.
30. "Pictures and Stage Totally Different," *New York Telegraph* (10 January 1915), p. 1D.
31. "Film Work Great for Actors," interview with Daniel Frohman, *New York Telegraph* (1 January 1915), p. 5.

Uncovering the Female Body

by Judith Mayne

Young Romance (Lasky, 1915), situated at the end of the "before Hollywood" era, offers an appropriate vantage point from which to ask questions about women in early cinema. A man and woman, strangers to each other, work in a department store: Tom in hardware, Nellie at the notions counter. Both nurture fantasies of romance and adventure, and they attempt to live out their fantasies by posing as wealthy, unattached socialites at a summer resort. Under their assumed identities, they meet and fall in love. At vacation's end, they separate—each fearful of being unmasked by the other. Only when they have returned to their real lives at the department store do they discover each other's true identity—and deception. All is forgiven, and the film concludes with a kiss.

Young Romance tells a story about the complications of fantasy. In that dream world, as in the cinema, men and women act out their fantasies in substantially different ways. From the film's beginning, it is clear that Tom's and Nellie's fantasies will lead them to each other. Nellie has planned hers far in advance: saving her money, arranging to stay in the best hotel, and even acquiring a suitable wardrobe of

second-hand clothes. To make her masquerade authentic, she even borrows the name of a wealthy store customer. Tom, on the other hand, has made no such plans; he simply leaves. Unlike Tom, Nellie knows how to create an image. In this sense, she is a quintessentially cinematic woman.

For feminist film critics, an understanding of women in the cinema has always focused on the question of image, a central concern in *Young Romance*. To speak of woman as image refers not simply to the representation of women in film (in this sense one speaks just as easily of images of men, for instance), but to the identification of women with the process of image making. What is striking about *Young Romance* is not so much its "images of woman," but rather the way in which the complications of the film develop so centrally from male and female identifications with the image. Nellie may invest more in the creation of her image than Tom does, but the investment backfires, in a sense, for Nellie is so successful at manipulating appearances that she attracts the attentions of a bankrupt count who kidnaps her

Enjoying a striptease in *Trapeze Disrobing Act* (1901).

Young Romance (1915).

Young Romance (1915).

in hopes of a huge ransom. This is where Tom intervenes: by not preparing his disguise as carefully as Nellie, he ends up staying at the same inexpensive boarding house as the count and thus discovers the count's evil plans. The plot thickens, in other words, around Nellie's excessive investment in her image and her rescue from excess by Tom.

If *image* in film means something different for women than for men, it may be because in film men are often the spectators and women the objects of spectacle. The question of image is ultimately a question of spectacle. Here, feminist critics have borrowed John Berger's description of the "surveyed female" in Western painting to describe how in film as in painting

. . . *men act* and *women appear*. Men look at women. Women watch themselves being looked at. This determines not only most relations between men and women but also the relation of women to themselves. The surveyor of woman in herself is male: the surveyed female. Thus she turns herself into an object—and most particularly an object of vision: a sight.[1]

Nellie is a "surveyed female" par excellence. If feminist critics have an investment in the images of women in the early cinema, then it is—to borrow from a 1903 title—a "search for evidence," for those moments that will make it possible, in 1915, for Tom and Nellie's story of young romance to take as its point of departure the differing relationships of men and women to image making.

One of the intriguing features of *Young Romance* is that the image Nellie adopts is shown, not just as a finished product, but as a process. For her image to be successful, a certain amount of work is required, and much of that work has to do with clothing. Indeed, the notion of woman's image always assumes a relationship between the female form and fashion, between the body and clothing which reveals and conceals.

How convenient, and appropriate, that in one of the earliest Edison films, *Annabelle Butterfly Dance* (1895), a woman's clothing plays a central role. Dancing for the camera, the woman is dressed in billowing fabric that swirls

Young Romance (1915).

Annabelle Butterfly Dance (1895).

Trapeze Disrobing Act (1901).

What Happened on Twenty-Third Street, New York City (1901).

about her, almost engulfing her at times. That the woman is performing for the camera is clear, but the movements of her body and the swirling fabric do not seem to be anchored in a specific context. The film could be taking place on a stage or in a studio. There is an *excess* in this short film, not the excess of identification as in *Young Romance*, but rather an excess of flowing movement; there is little distinction between the movements of the body and of the fabric. Put another way, the film, like the fabric, hides the female body while also displaying it. The simultaneous display and concealment could be read as a condition of the voyeuristic appeal of the cinema.

Another film, *Trapeze Disrobing Act* (Edison, 1901) suggests precisely that appeal. Two men, seated in a theater box, watch a woman strip while on a trapeze. There is little doubt about the intended audience for this spectacle, and there is little excess in the movements of the woman's body. In a very rudimentary and clear-cut way, the image of woman is created for male eyes: man is the subject, woman the object.

Can the relationship between *Butterfly Dance* and *Trapeze Disrobing Act* account for the cinema in its entirety? *Trapeze Disrobing Act* is, after all, a very obvious example. Consider another example, which may also be obvious, although perhaps in a more subtle and far-reaching way. *What Happened on Twenty-Third Street, New York City* (Edison, 1902) shows a city street, with people walking toward and away from the camera. As one woman approaches, she steps on a subway grate and her skirt billows upward: this action marks the end of the film, and provides a rudimentary narrative structure. The street is framed in such a way to suggest that the film screen is located on a fascinating boundary, between a real street, bustling with the activity of everyday life, and the fantasy space of fiction. The woman's body, now clad in street clothes, does nothing more than walk toward the camera. This movement appears limited when compared to the movements of the woman in *Butterfly Dance*. Similarly, the billowing fabric, which at times overwhelms the woman's body in *Butterfly Dance*, is suggested here as well in limited form, the single lift of the woman's skirts. The source of this movement is no longer the body itself, but a subway grate. Hence the woman's body is being restrained. In *Trapeze Disrobing Act*, that restraint is a function of spectacle; in *What Happened on Twenty-Third Street*, it is a function of narrative *and* spectacle—that is, of a story whose punchline is the sight of the female body caught unaware.

From *Butterfly Dance* to *Trapeze Disrobing Act* to *What Happened on Twenty-Third Street*, there is the progressive definition of woman as the object of spectacle, with clothing a symptom of that definition. If the swirling fabric of the butterfly dancer suggests that the movements of the female body are unrestricted, then the raised skirt of the woman in *What Happened on Twenty-Third Street* and the striptease-on-trapeze in *Trapeze Disrobing Act* are signs of a body meant to be scrutinized.

The implications of that scrutiny are taken a step further in *Uncle Josh at the Moving Picture Show* (Edison, 1903). Uncle Josh is a naive spectator who goes to the movies for the first time and sees three films. In the first, *Black Diamond Express*, a train approaches the camera. Uncle Josh, like the early film viewers who saw the Lumière film *L'Arrivée d'un Train*, is terrified by the approaching train and runs for cover. The second film, *Parisian Dancer*, offers him a more secure vantage point, but when the dancer appears on screen and flounces her skirts, Uncle Josh jumps on stage and dances along with the image. When the last film, *A Country Couple*, is shown, Josh tears down the screen in an attempt to rescue the damsel in distress. Uncle Josh may be naive, unable to distinguish between image and reality, but his naiveté reflects a fundamental truth of the cinema: the image of woman is his to consume.

It is only 1903, and already the cinema seems to have articulated a well-defined hierarchy of men looking and women being looked at. Indeed, *Uncle Josh at the Moving Picture Show* appears to be a perfect illustration of a feminist thesis. But at the same moment that the film illustrates the thesis, it complicates it. Uncle Josh also makes a spectacle of himself. If his gesture of tearing down the screen suggests an acting-out of the prerogatives of a male viewer, it is significant that the gesture occurs, not in response to an image of a woman, but to an image of a woman *and* a man. This is no simple fantasy of man possessing woman, but rather of child (Uncle Josh is a naive spectator, after all) and adult. Meanwhile, the Parisian dancer remains at a distance. Josh may dance with the image, but those flouncing skirts mark a boundary that even he does not transgress. Perhaps some of the swirling, excessive movements of the butterfly dancer are not so easily contained after all.

A feminist reading of the early cinema discovers structure, hierarchy, even conquest of the female body. At the same time there are moments, such as those in *Uncle Josh at the Moving Picture Show*, that resist the simplicity of the formula, "men act and women appear." Those moments suggest that the early cinema is no more easily reduced to a one-dimensional image than is the female body. If one stage of a feminist reading of early films involves a mapping-out of that fundamental structure whereby men look and women are looked at, a second stage seeks out the resistances to that formula, the complications and contradictions. That second stage is crucial, for to remain at the first stage is to resist any genuine encounter with the cinema, and, in essence, to regard with the cinema only in the terms defined by how, we assume, the cinema has regarded with women.

If one reading of women in the early cinema connects *Butterfly Dance* to *Trapeze Disrobing Act*, *What Happened on Twenty-Third Street*, and *Uncle Josh at the Moving Picture Show* in a linear progression, another reading might take *Uncle Josh at the Moving Picture Show* as a starting point. This second reading of early film pinpoints moments where the issues of image and spectacle, women and men, are not easily reducible to simplistic hierarchies. One such moment occurs in *What Happened in the Tunnel* (Edison, 1903). Two women, a white woman and her black maid, are riding in a train. When the train passes through a tunnel—a passage marked by a darkened screen—a male passenger attempts to steal a kiss from the white woman. Once the train has left the tunnel, he realizes—much to his chagrin—that he has kissed the maid. This film could be read in the terms we have already described, here with a racist twist. The man looks and wants to possess what he sees, but he kisses the "wrong" woman, the inappropriate object of spectacle.

What Happened in the Tunnel (1903).

What Happened in the Tunnel (1903).

However, if the two women in this film are objects of the male look, they turn the tables by laughing at the man. Metaphorically speaking their laughter, the film's punchline, suggests a flouncing skirt or a movement of the female body that resists the authority of the male look.

The encounter with the early cinema which I have described concerns a specific subject—women—and a specific critical mode—feminism. Even though "specialized," in the sense that any set of critical methods is, a feminist reading of the image of woman in early cinema underscores fundamental issues of what might be called the "readability" of early cinema. A relevant term here is one used by Russian formalist critic Victor Shklovsky to describe the function of art: "defamiliarization." Art defamiliarizes the objects and gestures to which we have become overly accustomed and therefore desensitized. Art renews and redefines perception by casting the familiar in new light.[2] Much of the fascination and pleasure associated with cinema in the early years had to do with the presentation of the familiar—a woman walking down a city street, for example—from a new vantage point, shaped by camera, screen, and spectator's seat.

For contemporary viewers, the realm of the familiar is constituted, at least in part, by the cinema itself. Early cinema defamiliarizes cinematic habits. The early "before"

Hollywood films are both familiar and strange, with moments of recognition and moments of confusion or perplexity. In some films, plots, patterns, and techniques are familiar, almost prefiguring what the cinema would become "after" Hollywood. Much work on the early cinema has emphasized those links between the "primitive" and the "mature" art form. But to assume that the early cinema will always reveal some truth about the cinema as we know it, is an oversimplification. We may see in the early cinema rudimentary forms of what the cinema has become; but there are many films which, for whatever reasons, resist such connections. For film critics of whatever persuasion, the challenge of the early cinema is to account both for the familiarity and the strangeness.

What would it mean to account for the early cinema in defamiliarized terms, that is, in relationship to our cinematic habits? That the early cinema and feminist criticism are allies in this venture was suggested to me recently as I watched an episode of a television program. In close-up, a man and a woman are discussing an evil plan, and their voices continue the discussion as we see them in long-shot, walking down a busy city street, toward the camera. The woman is conventionally beautiful and strikingly dressed. In long shot, what is most visible is her full skirt, which flutters and flies around her legs (it is a breezy day). As the couple approached he camera, I found myself ignoring the dialogue, and wondering if the scene's punchline might be a sudden gust of wind, exposing the woman's legs. Were I to suggest, in the name of feminist film criticism, that the real interest of this scene was the female body, clad and photographed in such a way to suggest the possibility of disrobement, I would surely be accused of "going too far." But my more immediate reaction was simply to remember *What Happened on Twenty-Third Street*, which is precisely "about" the female body caught unaware. Eighty years later, something of that scene lingers on in film (or television) viewing. An encounter with the early cinema makes us realize, perhaps, that there is something of Uncle Josh in all of us.

1. John Berger, *Ways of Seeing* (New York and London: Penguin Books & BBC, 1972), p. 47.
2. Victor Shklovsky, "Art as Technique," in Lee T. Lemon and Marion J. Reis, eds., *Russian Formalist Criticism: Four Essays* (Lincoln: University of Nebraska Press, 1965), pp. 3–25.

Dream Visions in Pre-Hollywood Film

by Russell Merritt

Hallucinations, nightmares, and visions in movies of the pre–World War I era have always attracted film writers through their liberating influence on narrative technique. Dream visions in all their various guises worked to free filmmakers from the constraints of orthodox storytelling strategies by authorizing the kind of logic that could exploit the mysterious effects of trick photography, unorthodox editing techniques, and peculiar lighting effects. Evolving from the simple trick films of Georges Méliès and Emile Cohl, the dream film represented an attempt to ground the film's action and special effects in a subjective point of view. A waiter's DTs are the excuse for the strange transformations in *The Hasher's Delirium* (Gaumont, 1910), a film replete with nonsequitur imagery, irrational juxtapositions, and strange transformations; the simple daydreams of an outcast newsboy trigger the slow-motion photography and stop-frame animation of *Bobby's Daydream* (Vitagraph, 1907). Whether a simple dream of wish fulfillment, as in *The Idler* (Pathé, 1907) in which a lazy man dreams and (through stop-frame animation) his household tasks perform themselves, or an indulgence-induced nightmare, as in *Dream of a*

Rarebit Fiend (Edison, 1906) which was constructed of superimpositions and model work, dreams function to authenticate a subjective point of view that has little to do with either the norms of conscious logic or the limitations of mundane reality. In these films, stop-frame animation, double exposure, reverse motion, and accelerated or retarded motion, along with other manipulations achieved in the camera or in printing, render the hectic fantasies of the dreamer.

The survey of films represented in the *Before Hollywood* exhibition features several noteworthy examples of stories structured around the logic of dreams and told from the dreamer's point of view. The period covered in this program was a remarkably fertile one, and the dream vision represents its most consistently self-reflexive form of theatrical filmmaking—the genre that comments directly on film's innards, inviting the audience to study the medium's peculiar representation/misrepresentation of life.

Perhaps the most important thing to note about this

A nightmare ride in *The Dream of a Rarebit Fiend* (1906).

Princess Nicotine; or, The Smoke Fairy (1909).

Princess Nicotine; or, The Smoke Fairy (1909).

oftmade point is that this role is deliberately and self-consciously assumed. The spectator is never permitted to forget that a theatrical performance is being observed. The dreamer is the center of attention and like his predecessors—the magician in the Méliès *films truc* and the sketch artist in early animation films—he is the on-screen presence who creates and then beholds his own magical, impossible creation.[1] The audience recognizes from the story framing the dream that a mundane situation is about to be transformed, and when the dream vision springs to life, the dreamer frequently acts as a surrogate for the audience, admiring or being dazzled by the special effects.

The almost obsessive desire to reveal the mechanics of trick photography to the audience, recalling the playful demonstrations of animated photography in Winsor Mc-Cay's cartoons, should be apparent to anyone leafing through the pages of trade journals of the day. In contrast to the magician's code of secrecy, these films revel in making known their secrets. *Princess Nicotine* (Vitagraph, 1909), an American imitation of Emile Cohl's *Les Allumettes Animées* released by Gaumont a year earlier, was the subject of a lengthy article in the *Nickelodeon* that explained ("through the kindness of Mr. J. Stuart Blackton and Mr. Albert E. Smith of the Vitagraph Company") the mysteries of the film's stop-motion photography, split-screen effects, and use of mattes.[2] For *A Mid-Winter's Night Dream* (Vitagraph, 1906), one of the countless variations of Hans Christian

Andersen's story, "The Little Match Girl," Blackton and Smith prepared a press release that exposed the secrets of the special effects photography that animates the teddy bear, monkey, and tabletop toys. By 1909, *Moving Picture World* had a regular column on the latest developments in trick photography. If, as Donald Crafton has written in his illuminating history of animated film, the earliest producers of trick films stimulated public interest by intentionally creating an atmosphere of mystery in keeping technology secret, by 1907 this policy had been permanently reversed.[3] Special effects predate movie personalities as the earliest film stars, becoming the focus of the film companies' original publicity campaigns.

The self-reflexive, self-promoting aspect of dream films help to explain the peculiar way the representations of dreams evolved in silent cinema. As post-Freudians, we might expect these films to represent an early interest in human psychology and to evolve into increasingly sophisticated studies of the human subconscious. But in America this is precisely what did not happen. Instead, the dream conventions were continually combined with other formulas—most frequently the comic chase film, the patriotic or religious pageant, Western, crime thriller, or Arabian Nights romance—to fashion a burlesque or didactic parable. Biograph's *Terrible Ted* (1907), one of the most exhilarating dream films, takes on the bloodthirsty conventions of the dime novels and the country's ongoing love affair with Teddy

Teddy Roosevelt shoots a cat in *Terrible Teddy, the Grizzly King* (1901).

Ted stabs a bear in *Terrible Ted* (1907).

Roosevelt; its exuberant eleven-year-old protagonist dreams up grandiose rescues, shoot-outs, a bear fight, and gory Indian massacres before getting his comeuppance. In Vitagraph's *And the Villain Still Pursued Her* (1906), we watch a hack theater writer hoist on his own petard, caught up in a comic nightmare drawn from the melodramatic clichés of bad "sensation drama." *The Dream* (IMP, 1911), another comic nightmare, uses the dream framework to recycle a vaudeville character type that Mary Pickford and others had already tried on the screen with great success—the boisterous, willful housewife.

But perhaps the most glaring feature of the dream film is the persistent undercurrent of ethical and social didacticism implicit within the vision. From the start, producers were encouraged to reveal moral truths within their dream fantasies, unlike the earlier trick films, which seldom pointed to specific moral lessons. Sleep and a guilty conscience conspire to create nightmares that effect permanent reform in the protagonist's waking life; overindulgence in food, tobacco, and (especially) alcohol lead to hallucinations so scary or bewildering that the dreamer swears off all further

reveal the pleasures of the unfettered imagination and to repeat on all-powerful commandment—"Don't!"[4]

This characteristic moralizing sharply differentiates American from European dream films and may explain the reluctance of American producers to present fantasies outside the dream framework. For all their fascination with dreams, American producers confined them with clearly defined boundaries. Fantasy was to be distinguished from, subordinated to, and made dependent upon the waking world. The dream, like the theatrical performance, was to guide its beholder to more sensible living; however mad the logic, it was to be contained within the rational boundaries of the real world by clearly marked transitional devices. Whereas French filmmakers such as Emile Cohl and Louis Feuillade quickly discarded the dream frame to create free-floating, almost plotless chains of images, Americans made their dream frames more elaborate and expanded the moral spectacle. Rather than move inward to explore the psychological relationships between dream and reality, Americans moved outward to mount grandiose dream visions.

Most commonly, from about 1910 to 1929, the dream

The Dream (1911).

The Kid (1921).

binges. Daydreams of happy homes, peaceful kingdoms, and honest employers are presented as comments on the hard realities of the outside world.

In function and overall structure, these dream films closely resemble another narrative form gaining popularity at the time—the drama-within-a-film, which almost invariably points to the salutary, moral effect of dramatic arts. In movies of this sort, the protagonist watches a play, vaudeville sketch, amateur theatrical, or movie and learns a lesson of great worth. In each case, the theatrical performance, like the dream, is an agent of reform, holding a mirror up to the spectator-protagonist that reveals the heartlessness of divorce, the evils of liquor, or the folly of infidelity.

In some cases, dreams are not so overtly didactic. *Terrible Ted*, for example, owes part of its charm and startling freshness to its refusal to deliver a homily. Even in such films, however, dreams invariably comment on moral virtues, a tendency that has proven remarkably durable. What Maxine Gorky wrote of the American amusement park is true of the dream in the American dream film. The fantastical spectacle, he observed, has a divided purpose: to

became a kind of allegory that suggested an all-knowing, supernatural narrative voice, endowed with Olympian infallible perception to illustrate eternal verities. Dream allegories in silent comedies are probably the most familiar to us: the famous "heaven" sequence, for instance, in Charlie Chaplin's *The Kid* (First National, 1921), in which Chaplin, having lost Jackie Coogan, dreams that his shabby courtyard has become celestially embowered with flowers and angels and peopled with comic symbols named Innocence and Temptation; or, the Satyr-like frolic among nymphs in *Sunnyside* (First National, 1918).

But the dream vision was to become no less common in dramatic films where it was frequently intertwined with allegorical and supernatural figures. Midway through *Sparrows* (United Artists, 1926), for instance, Mary Pickford's character dozes off in an attic, holding a dying baby in her arms. A picture of Jesus Christ materializes on the back wall of the attic, part of a pastoral tableau vivant. Jesus steps out of the picture, comes forward to take the dead baby out of Mary's arms, and then returns into the tableau as the picture disappears. In *Hell's Hinges* (Triangle, 1916), William S.

Hart daydreams about his sweetheart as he hears her sing with the church choir. He closes his eyes, and the image of his sweetheart singing appears. This, in turn, dissolves into the image of a woman, clinging to a cross, atop a sea-swept rock—a scene presumably representing the hymn his sweetheart sings: Thomas Hasting's "Rock of Ages."

Conversely, the allegorical tableau of the nineteenth-century stage was modified to blend into the dream format. The explicit allegories that served as the finales for such films as *The Birth of a Nation* (Epoch Producing Corporation, 1915), and *Intolerance* (Work Producing Corporation, 1916) soon gave way to personal visions, rooted in subjective points of view. So, the introduction of the allegorical horsemen in Rex Ingram's film *Four Horsemen of the Apocalypse* (Metro, 1921), is framed by a bearded stranger telling a bewildered Rudolph Valentino his version of the biblical prophecy. The allegory has been made a personal vision emanating from a single consciousness. Biblical and historical pageants became a fixture in Cecil B. DeMille's films, following the success of *Joan the Woman* (Lasky, 1917). But even when these historical sequences were introduced as simple analogies to certain aspects of the modern narratives, as in *Male and Female* (Artcraft, 1919) or *The Ten Commandments* (Lasky, 1923), they were invariably moored to the modern dramas by framing devices—a character reading from a book, for instance, or recounting a fabulous dream. The Olympian, omniscient perspective of *Intolerance*, which collated four disparate stories with an image of universal motherhood, was rapidly eclipsed by presentational devices that authorized historical flashbacks as renderings of dreams, readings, or imaginings.

This tradition of the dream vision retarded any systematic study of the dream itself on film (to my knowledge, there were no American equivalents to *The Secrets of the Soul* or *Fragment of an Empire*), but as early dream films illustrate, the dream vision created the occasion for witty, sometimes brilliant dramatic economies that freed directors from the demands of photographic and narrative realism.

1. For the best description of the lightning-sketch act as the seminal form of American film animation, see Donald Crafton, *Before Mickey* (Cambridge, Mass.: MIT Press, 1982), pp. 48–57.
2. L. Gardette, "Some Tricks of the Moving Picture Maker," *The Nickelodeon* 2 (August 1909), p. 53.
3. Crafton, *Before Mickey*, pp. 17–18, 30–31.
4. Maxine Gorky, "Boredom," *The Independent* (8 August 1907), p. 313.

Photography/Cinematography

by Alan Trachtenberg

"The ideal film," remarked Vachel Lindsay in his incomparable 1915 tract of prophecy and fantasy, *The Art of the Moving Picture*, "has no rewards printed on it at all, but is one unbroken sheet of photography."[1] The image is jolting: an unbroken sheet of *photography*? Unfamiliar and jarring, Lindsay's association of cinema with the photograph brings us back to the essential nature of the movies: cinema consists of a linear sequence of *still* photographic images, each differing in slight degree from the next and together creating the illusion of motion. Movement out of stillness is the paradoxical fact of the medium. Moreover the illusion of motion succeeds because the individual photographic image becomes invisible. The viewer cannot single out a particular still—a paradoxical and a well-concealed fact. This is an ironic casualty, so to speak, of that illusion of reality, that immediacy of representation, which is the camera's singular bequest to the art of the moving picture.

The relation of photography to cinematography in the emergence and shaping of cinema has not been carefully examined, and the exhibition of these early films from the so-called primitive era affords a special view. Cinema arose from the conjunction of two products of technology: (1) a device that presented a series of images so rapidly that there was an illusion of continuous motion, based on the phenomenon of "afterimage;" and (2) an apparatus for projecting such continuous pictures. So far, photography proper plays no essential role. The projected images might well be hand-drawn on a translucent ground. However, while there is no inherent reason for the image to be photographic, cinema without photography is almost unimaginable. By trying to imagine it, we can better appreciate the role played by photography in the emergence of the cinema.

The question of photography's role in motion picture history concerns cinema as an artifact made under particular circumstances. It is a question of form and of aesthetic analysis. As always, however, form remains inseparable from content, and aesthetics is inextricably entangled with history. Photography is not merely the camera apparatus. It is also the entire system of picture-making practices:

Reviewing photographs of suitors in *A Tin-Type Romance* (1910).

Early photographers documented faraway places: Chusseau Flavien's "Scene at the Pyramids" (ca. 1895).

Tourists snap photos in *Ancient Temples of Egypt* (1912).

the subjects chosen; the photographer's aims, commercial or artistic; and the modes of representation such as the code of perspective, which governs two-dimensional imitation of deep space. Photography denotes a process of *making meaning* through pictures. By the 1890s, this cultural process had infiltrated the entire society, establishing itself as perhaps the prime arbiter of "reality."

As Lindsay well understood, the infant art of moving pictures drew its lifeblood from photography and the general visual culture in which photography played a leading role. Indeed, as the earliest films often so charmingly and

intelligently reveal, a lively symbiosis joined the two mediums. The industrialized urban societies of the nineteenth century seemed obsessed with visual aids. Binoculars, opera glasses, and scopes of all sorts, as well as devices for specular illusion such as dioramas, panoramas, stereopticon and lantern slide projections, all gained tremendous popularity. Technologies of vision, not confined to photography, provided a matrix for the new moving pictures and animated illusions. Photography itself proved the most consequential of these technologies. It offered a way of seeing and explaining commonplace experiences. In city views and

View of lower Manhattan from *The European Rest Cure* (1904).

street scenes, everyday life took on a new immediacy, often without the controls and mediations of pictorial composition.

Photography as narrative also anticipated cinema. From the earliest years, photographers sought to combine pictures into sequences for the sake of telling stories. As early as the 1840s, photography's first decade, there were sequences of images, protonarratives of, say, a game of chess or a heated conversation. Staged tableaux vivants, which were standard fare of Victorian photography, developed into the so-called sentimentals. These narrative sequences, often racy and wanton, were produced by the stereocard industry. Yet another popular diversion was the making of photo albums, usually centering on family life, with pictures of places as well as people. The family album invariably told a rambling but coherent story. Albums devoted to special occasions—a tour of the Holy Land, a visit to Rome— were not merely records but also narratives, no matter how naive and plotless.

Far from naive, on the other hand, were the fascinating and little-known experiments by Alexander Black in 1894 and 1895, exactly on the threshold of cinema. In what he called "picture plays," sequences of stills were projected on a screen upon a stage. The stills illustrated a story that was simultaneously read aloud from the same stage. In two of his productions, subsequently published as illustrated fictions, Black explored narrative devices such as continuity editing and montage.[2] He took care with staging and lighting, and made a point of including well-known living personages, portraying themselves, along with fictive roles performed by actors, thus "bringing [to life] the living characters of fictitious action against the actual life of the city."[3] Remarkably knowing and articulate, Black explained in prefatory notes that the "effect of reality" could not be achieved by "isolated pictures" but required "the blending of many," "which was a protocinematic conception. He described his work as "the art of the tableau vivant plus the science of photography," a staging plus a recording. While art's task was "to translate nature," the "privilege of photography" was to transmit nature."[4] This fusion of science and art was essential for the photoplay, because, he wrote, "the literal is not always the highest truth." He noted "widely divergent ways of transmitting a fact" and sought to create "the illusion that the thing seen is something that is happening or actually has happened in an actual room." Creating "the

effect of reality" is paramount: as Black explained, "The photographer is in a disappointing business when he devotes himself to making his very pretty Rhine stone look like a real diamond."[5]

Preferring the rhinestone *as it is*, its real prettiness against a fake brilliance, Black speaks in the language of "realism," a way of thinking about art and life as well as a set of conventions for representing the world. His mode of thought and practice seemed naturally akin to photography. "In recording literal fact the painter cannot draw like the camera," wrote Black, "for no eye has the truth of a good lens."[6] This idea pervaded modern culture by the turn of the century; it was a mode of consciousness founded upon a cultural belief in the mechanical reproducibility of all real things—of reality itself—and in the truth of photographs.

A mere ghost in an emulsion, the photographic image proved capable of adhering to any surface—to glass as easily as wood or paper—and it insinuated itself everywhere. By the 1890s, the term *photographic* implied ease of transfer, interchangeability, as well as mechanical reproduction. A new way of representing what is real, the photograph was itself something new. The emulsified image made an extraordinary difference in how reality was understood; the emulsion was capable of rematerializing as an image, almost instantaneously, in defiance of time, space, and mass. On the threshold of cinematography, then, the realm of photography was already established as the realm of free-floating, emulsified images. Not "pictures," properly speaking, photographs performed their work in society in similar ways, as depictions of the real.

The belief in a pure photographic truth is worse than naive; photography becomes an instrument of deceptions. Still, taken simply as a kind of communication, a signifying field, the photograph *is* relatively free of overt signs of interference from an editorializing hand. The photograph does compel its viewer to contemplate what seems an authentic token of reality, teaching viewers to read signs of life in black and white. Photography helped engender a new visibility in things and contributed to a rise in visibility itself. A high value was placed upon sight and its uses in modern culture—from surveillance to survey to spectacle to art. More intensely and urgently than in the past, to see became to know—or to hope to know.

And this uniquely modern conflation of vision and knowledge lay at the basis, at least as Vachel Lindsay insisted, of the art of moving pictures. Lindsay wanted "no words" in his ideal film because pictures possessed the voice of "our new picture alphabets." Indeed long before Roland Barthes' remark that cinema speaks in a "purely gestural vocabulary," Lindsay introduced the notion of "Photoplay Hieroglyphics" as the essential signifying element in film. Such hieroglyphics might well achieve that same precision of meaning found in the ancient Egyptian prototypes. For example, in ancient texts a picture of a window, with closed shutters is the equivalent of the Latin *P*: a coincidence Lindsay interprets as meaning that the "Intimate Photoplay" itself "is but a window where we open the shutters and peep into someone's cottage."[7] Lindsay employs the term *hieroglyphic* as a trope for visual interpretation, for the deciphering of pictures in general. "A tribe that has thought in words since the days that it worshiped Thor and told legends of the cunning of the tongue of Loki," he wrote, "suddenly begins to think in pictures."[8] Thus the moving picture heralds an altogether new moment in cultural history.

Lindsay's observation that "American civilization grows more and more hieroglyphic every day," might well be confirmed by a close look at the photographic hieroglyphics worked into early films to provide moments of scrutiny and scrutability.[9] Such instances can tell us much about the photography/cinematography symbiosis. Most often the photographs glimpsed in early films are portraits, serving to identify or unmask false identities, as in *The Ranchman's Rival* (Essanay, 1909), in which the already married pretender is undone by an old photograph. In *The Girl of the Golden West* (Lasky, 1915), the question of the identity of Ramerrez is settled by the studio photo that the jilted and vindictive Nina slips to Rance. In this photo the outlaw is intentionally shown posing as a conventional romantic cowboy, a guise that proves almost true at the end, the photograph thereby complicating the question of identity. In *How Men Propose* (Crystal, 1913) the sly young lady gives away her own game, at the expense of her several suitors, by bestowing upon each an identical photograph of herself. In other instances a photograph serves as a surrogate person by which a character, and the viewer, can measure changes in a relationship. In *The Passer-By* (Edison, 1912), a framed photograph of the storyteller's old sweetheart reminds him of the betrayal that launched his decline; the framed portrait of the same lady, now a society matron, looms behind him on the wall of the gentleman's club where he recounts his pathetic tale, a token for him and for us of the terrible irony of that moment of recognition. An extreme example of a photograph substituting for reality is in *The Dream* (IMP, 1911), where the reformed profligate passionately tears up the picture of his adulterous sweetheart, a symbolic gesture of reformation. Just as extreme, although in a vein of comic foolishness, are the histrionics in the game of exchanging locket tin-types in *A Tin-Type Romance* (Vitagraph, 1910).

Photography uncovers the truth astonishingly in *The Story the Biograph Told* (Biograph, 1903) in which the camera is a moving camera and the picture is not a photograph but a film. The story revolves around the making of a film within the film. An unsuspecting married businessman, unaware that a mischievous office boy is recording his antics with a motion picture camera, flirts with his compliant secretary. Later, the philanderer's wife sees the office boy's film, discovering her husband's infidelity and soon putting a stop to his pleasures. This curiously self-reflexive little film is also the occasion for striking cinematographic innovations: double-exposure is used to show both ends of a telephone conversation simultaneously; the main scene is refilmed, this time from behind the couple, to replicate the point of view of the on-screen camera.

On the whole these are fairly simple situations, and the photograph plays an apparently uncomplicated role. People in the films act as though photographs were reliable pieces of evidence, yet in so doing they are interpreting the picture, bringing to life an inert image. Are the pictures in these films reliable and one-dimensionally referential? Does the studio portrait tell the full story about Ramerrez; does it reveal who he is? In fact, a good number of these early films

The Girl of the Golden West (1915).

Standing before the portrait in *The Passer-By* (1912).

The Dream (1911).

A Tin-Type Romance (1910).

Getting Evidence (1906).

The Story the Biograph Told (1904).

The Story the Biograph Told (1904).

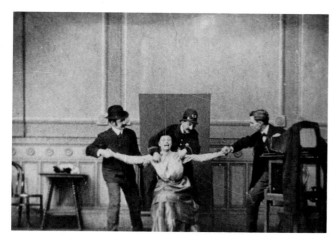

Photographing a Female Crook (1904).

concern themselves precisely with disguises, impersonations, deceit, betrayal, trickery, and pretense. Such films depict a comic world in which the acts of unmasking and reestablishing of social order are often central, and the reading of a photograph frequently provides the catalyst for such a corrective act. But reality often remains elusive and appearances ambiguous. Consider *Getting Evidence* (Edison, 1906), in which a gumshoe is retained to keep an eye presumably on an errant wife. He decides to use a camera, a decision fraught with danger for himself and laughs for the viewers. In the end, it is a case of mistaken identity, the detective-photographer in pursuit of the wrong party. While the film does not call into question the validity of the camera as an instrument for "getting evidence," it does portray the photographer as a buffoon, whose disguises and gaucheries make him the butt of the joke. It is as if the photographic eye, the prying eye of the surrogate authority figure, undergoes exorcism here. In the mockery, the image itself loses some of its authority, as it also does in the behind-the-scenes view of mug-shots being made in *Photographing a Female Crook* (Biograph, 1904). The crook in question resists with all her might, making faces at the studio camera, refusing to allow a clear view of her physiognomy, all the while the movie camera moves steadily toward her in a close-up. The moving picture seems to be wresting authority from the still picture.

The prominence of still photographs and photographers in these early movies may signify a kind of homage from the younger to the older medium, perhaps even a covert acknowledgment that still photographs are at the heart of film. The actual photographs embedded within the mise-en-scène symbolize a visual culture shared by photography and cinema in film's earliest years. For example, the moving-picture street scenes seem at times like Alfred Stieglitz's photographs of such subjects as horse-drawn street cars in the snow. At other times they call to mind Lewis Hine's scenes of Lower East Side streets brought to life. Such resemblances point to other transactions between the mediums, as when early films appeared as components of variety shows, often sharing the bill with lantern projections of still photographs.

The Strenuous Life; or, Anti-Race Suicide (1904).

Alfred Stieglitz's photograph *The Terminal* (1892).

Developing in the shadow of photography, moving pictures defined themselves willy-nilly by reference to their opposite. Indeed it was routine to project the opening shot of a film as a still image, which the film would then bring to life, activated as if by magic. This practice openly declared the symbiosis of still and moving photographs, acknowledg-

ing the still as the buried but essential component of film. The germinal image of each cinematic scene is nothing more than a single still photograph from which the whole scene springs. Every scene interprets its own still image—the originating hieroglyph—in an effort to make sense by exploring the still's dynamic implications. As Béla Balázs explained, "Pictures have no tenses. They show only the present—they cannot express either a past or a future tense. In a picture itself there is nothing that would compellingly and precisely indicate the reason for the picture being what it is."[10] Cinema responds to the atemporality of each still picture by supplying narrative flow, embedding individual pictures within an explanatory structure. In short, every still photograph implies both a spatial and temporal edge where what is not depicted in the image becomes present to it. Every still implies motion. The stopped action might continue, and the story unfold in any direction.

But it is not motion alone that constitutes the art of moving pictures. Photography reproduces the world by abstracting from it, freezing time and space. Cinematography reconstructs; in Eisenstein's words, it is "organization by means of the camera." Assembling its lexicon of devices from other media—mise-en-scène from theater, the fade or dissolve from the stereopticon, the cut from albums and from picture-stories such as those by Alexander Black—cinematography nevertheless produces a new artifact. Its aim is to create an illusion of total reality—to eliminate all signs of artifice and present a perfectly autonomous and self-generated world. In cinema, viewers are encouraged to leave their critical sense of artifice at the gate, to bring nothing into the darkened chamber with the silver screen but the capacity to surrender and to believe.

Certainly in its role as instrument of realism and arbiter of reality, photography governed cinema's quest for that illusion of reality. ("With the certain perfecting of orthochromatic photography and chronophotography," wrote inventor C. Francis Jenkins in 1898, "the means for recording the physical phenomena of nature and life will be complete.")[11] What photography itself helps us see in the early films is a cinematography still in the grip of older artifices, of modes and styles soon to be surpassed. On the whole, they derive from theater and take the form of painted sets and exaggerated histrionics, both of which are perfectly at home on stage. The proscenium itself declares the rule of pretense; the temporariness of the setting and backdrops, the unreality of role playing on stage. No one confuses the actor with his role, and if so, the confusion is not permitted to survive curtain calls and bows at the end.

Reproduced as moving pictures, such devices seem stilted, incongruous, and exposed as false. Cinematography endows settings as well as persons with the air of immediacy and actuality, and if an actor seems to be a melodramatic character actor, so be it—the rhinestone, not the fake diamond, paint seen as paint. Erwin Panofsky speaks of "that curious consubstantiality that exists between the person of the movie actor and his role,"[12] which is precisely the effect of photography within cinematography. It was this power of making an image seem real and present that early cinema impressed upon both its audience and its experimental practitioners at the same time.

Hugo Munsterberg evoked just this capacity when he

The Black Hand (1906).

wrote in 1916 that "the true field for the photoplay is the practical life which surrounds us, as no artistic means of literature or drama can render the details of life with such convincing sincerity and with such realistic power. These are the slums, not seen through the spectacles of a littérateur or the fancy of an outsider but in their whole abhorrent nakedness. These are the dark corners of the metropolis where crime is hidden and where vice grows rankly."[13] We have fleeting but compelling glimpses of such contemporary scenes as these in the early films: in *What Happened on Twenty-Third Street* (Edison, 1901), the camera is stationed on a sidewalk and creates its own subject; in the American Mutoscope and Biograph dramas, *The Skyscrapers of New York* (1906) and *The Tunnel Worker* (1906), there are astonishing scenes of workers at their worksites; and in several early Biograph films, notably *The Black Hand* (1905) and *The Romance of a Jewess* (1908), brief unstaged views of crowded lower Manhattan streets taken with a hidden camera are knit into melodramas otherwise staged upon the usual painted sets.

Such glimpses of a world captured and organized by the camera help to identify cinematographic potentialities in the new medium—what Lindsay meant by "an unbroken sheet of photography." Photography in all its guises helps us see this—photography as technique, theme, trope, and artifact within films. Even what is falsified stands revealed for what it is before the lens. In cinema's earliest decade, as perhaps

never again, photography brings incongruity into focus and thereby serves as the perspective in which the future of cinematography becomes clear.

1. Vachel Lindsay, *The Art of the Moving Picture* (New York: Liveright, 1970, p. 14.
2. Alexander Black, "Photography in Fiction," *Scribners*, 18 (September 1895), pp. 348–60; idem., "The Camera and the Comedy," *Scribner's*, 20 (November 1896), pp. 605–10; idem., *Time and Chance* (New York: Farrar and Rinehart, 1937), pp. 129–57. See also Burnes St. Patrick Hollyman, "Alexander Black's Picture Plays, 1893–1894," in *Film Before Griffith*, ed. John Fell (Berkeley: University of California Press, 1983), 236–43.
3. Black, "Photography in Fiction," p. 348.
4. Black, "The Camera and Comedy," p. 607–608.
5. Ibid.
6. Lindsay, p. 205.
7. Ibid., p. 213.
8. Ibid., p. 21–22.
9. Béla Balász, *Theory of Film* (New York: Dover, 1970), pp. 120–21.
10. C. Francis Jenkens, *Animated Pictures* (Washington, D.C.: 1898), p. vi.
11. Hans Panofsky, "Style and Medium in the Motion Pictures," in *Film Theory and Criticism*, eds. Gerald Mast and Marshall Cohen (New York: Oxford University Press 1974), p. 166.
12. Hugo Munsterberg, *The Film: A Psychological Study: The Silent Photoplay in 1916* (New York: Dover, 1970), p. 92.

Programs

Program 1: An Age of Entertainments

ANNABELLE BUTTERFLY DANCE
(Edison Manufacturing Company, 1895)

ANNABELLE SERPENTINE DANCE
(Edison Manufacturing Company, 1895)

FIRE RESCUE
(Edison Manufacturing Company, 1894)

SHOOTING THE CHUTES
(Edison Manufacturing Company, 1896)

MARKET SQUARE, HARRISBURG, PA.
(Edison Manufacturing Company, 1897)

RAILWAY STATION SCENE
(International Film Company, 1897)

THE PASSION PLAY OF OBERAMMERGAU (SELECT SCENES)
(Eden Musée, 1898)
"Salome's Dance"
"The Messiah's Entry into Jerusalem"
"The Ascension"

THE BATTLE OF MANILA BAY
(American Vitagraph Company, 1898)

SOLDIERS AT PLAY
(William Selig, 1898)

RAISING OLD GLORY OVER MORRO CASTLE
(American Vitagraph Company, 1899)

BLACKTON SKETCHING EDISON
(Edison Manufacturing Company, 1896)

BURGLAR ON THE ROOF
(American Vitagraph Company, 1898)

A VISIT TO THE SPIRITUALIST
(American Vitagraph Company, 1899)

THE TRAMP'S DREAM
(Sigmund Lubin, 1899)

SEARCHING RUINS ON BROADWAY, GALVESTON, FOR DEAD BODIES
(American Vitagraph Company, 1900)

SCENES OF THE WRECKAGE FROM THE WATERFRONT
(Sigmund Lubin, 1900)

BEHEADING THE CHINESE PRISONER
(Sigmund Lubin, 1900)

HOW THEY ROB MEN IN CHICAGO
(American Mutoscope and Biograph Company, 1900)

AN UNEXPECTED KNOCKOUT
(American Mutoscope and Biograph Company, 1901)

HE FORGOT HIS UMBRELLA
(American Mutoscope and Biograph Company, 1901)

A MIGHTY TUMBLE
(American Mutoscope and Biograph Company, 1901)

NEXT!
(American Mutoscope and Biograph Company, 1903)

SMASHING A JERSEY MOSQUITO
(Edison Manufacturing Company, 1902)

THE BURNING OF DURLAND'S RIDING ACADEMY
(Edison Manufacturing Company, 1902)

ELECTROCUTING AN ELEPHANT
(Edison Manufacturing Company, 1903)

WHAT HAPPENED ON TWENTY-THIRD STREET, NEW YORK CITY
(Edison Manufacturing Company, 1901)

TRAPEZE DISROBING ACT
(Edison Manufacturing Company, 1901)

WHAT HAPPENED IN THE TUNNEL
(Edison Manufacturing Company, 1903)

THE STORY THE BIOGRAPH TOLD
(American Mutoscope and Biograph Company, 1904)

PULL DOWN THE CURTAINS, SUZIE
(American Mutoscope and Biograph Company, 1904)

MEET ME AT THE FOUNTAIN
(Sigmund Lubin, 1904)

RUBE AND MANDY AT CONEY ISLAND
(Edison Manufacturing Company, 1903)

THE EUROPEAN REST CURE
(Edison Manufacturing Company, 1904)

THE STRENUOUS LIFE; OR, ANTI-RACE SUICIDE
(Edison Manufacturing Company, 1904)

THE SUBURBANITE
(American Mutoscope and Biograph Company, 1904)

Program 2: Pleasures and Pitfalls

INTERIOR N.Y. SUBWAY, 14TH STREET TO 42ND STREET
(American Mutoscope and Biograph Company, 1905)

CONEY ISLAND AT NIGHT
(Edison Manufacturing Company, 1905)

THE HOLD-UP OF THE ROCKY MOUNTAIN EXPRESS
(American Mutoscope and Biograph Company, 1906)

THE MILLER'S DAUGHTER
(Edison Manufacturing Company, 1905)

GETTING EVIDENCE
(Edison Manufacturing Company, 1906)

PHOTOGRAPHING A FEMALE CROOK
(American Mutoscope and Biograph Company, 1904)

THE BLACK HAND
(American Mutoscope and Biograph Company, 1906)

TERRIBLE TED
(American Mutoscope and Biograph Company, 1907)

FOUL PLAY; OR, A FALSE FRIEND
(Vitagraph Company of America, 1906)

THE THIEVING HAND
(Vitagraph Company of America, 1908)

THE UNWRITTEN LAW: A THRILLING DRAMA
BASED ON THE THAW-WHITE CASE
(Sigmund Lubin, 1907)

THREE AMERICAN BEAUTIES
(Edison Manufacturing Company, 1906)

Program 3: America in Transition

FIRST MAIL DELIVERY BY AEROPLANE
(Powers, 1911)

ANCIENT TEMPLES OF EGYPT
(Kalem Company, 1912)

PRINCESS NICOTINE; OR, THE SMOKE FAIRY
(Vitagraph Company of America, 1909)

A TIN-TYPE ROMANCE
(Vitagraph Company of America, 1910)

A FRIENDLY MARRIAGE
(Vitagraph Company of America, 1911)

THE USURER
(Biograph Company, 1910)

WINNING AN HEIRESS
(Essanay Film Manufacturing Company, 1911)

THE DREAM
(Independent Moving Picture Company, 1911)

THE INFORMER
(Biograph Company, 1912)

Program 4: Domestic Life

THE OLD ACTOR
(Biograph Company, 1912)

THE PASSER-BY
(Edison Manufacturing Company, 1912)

THE WATER NYMPH
(Keystone Company, 1912)

ONE IS BUSINESS; THE OTHER CRIME
(Biograph Company, 1912)

HOW MEN PROPOSE
(Crystal, 1913)

A HOUSE DIVIDED
(Solax, 1913)

THE VAMPIRE
(Kalem Company, 1913)

Program 5: The Frontier Spirit

MAIDEN AND MEN
(American Film Manufacturing Company, 1912)

THE RUSE
(New York Motion Picture Company, 1915)

THE GIRL OF THE GOLDEN WEST
(Jesse L. Lasky Feature Play Company, 1915)

Program 6: Love and Misadventure

DREAMY DUD: HE RESOLVES NOT TO SMOKE
(Essanay Company, 1915)

WHO PAYS?
Episode Seven: "Blue Blood and Yellow"
(Balboa Amusement Company, 1915)

YOUNG ROMANCE
(Jesse L. Lasky Feature Play Company, 1915)

Program I: An Age of Entertainments

The Story the Biograph Told (1904).

Annabelle Butterfly Dance

1895. Edison Manufacturing Company. Distributed by Maguire and Baucus and their Continental Commerce Company.
Photographed by W.K.L. Dickson and William Heise. With Annabelle Moore. Shot at Edison's Black Maria studio in
West Orange, New Jersey, in early 1895. Print source: American Film Institute. 19 sec.

Looking at *Annabelle* today, so many years after it was
made, one is struck by how much, and how little, we can
see. She neither enters nor exits, and there is no suggestion
of any world beyond the borders of the frame. Annabelle
Moore and her flowing drapes dominate the screen space.
Turning, crouching, extending her arms, carving this space
with this "costume" that magnifies her gestures (Annabelle
Moore's dance is clearly an imitation of Loie Fuller), Annabelle exists in an artificial space that makes no reference
to the stage or anything else, except possibly a photographer's studio. On the other hand, she certainly does acknowledge the camera lens. This is no accident. *Annabelle*
was filmed in the Black Maria, a tiny studio that was
functionally an extension of Edison's kinetograph motion
picture camera. Only a few people could appear before the
lens—isolated before a black background. The only audience was the camera operator; the camera, bolted to the
floor, did not move. Filming began and ended with no
editing to arrange the images.   —Robert Haller

Annabelle Serpentine Dance

1895. Edison Manufacturing Company. Distributed by Maguire and Baucus and their Continental Commerce Company.
Photographed by W.K.L. Dickson and William Heise. With Annabelle Moore. Shot at Edison's Black Maria studio
in West Orange, New Jersey, in early 1895. Print source: Museum of Modern Art. 27 sec.

The first commercially successful motion picture projector in the United States was invented by C. Francis Jenkins and Thomas Armat. However, in its best-known incarnation, the vitascope, it was generally promoted as the invention of Thomas Edison. —Charles Musser

LIFELESS SKIRT DANCERS
In Gauzy Silks They Smirk and
Pirouette at Wizard Edison's Command

"For the first time since Edison has been working on his new invention, the vitascope, persons other than his trusted employees and assistants were allowed last night to see the workings of the wonderful machine. For two hours dancing girls and groups of figures all of life size, seemed to exist as realities on the big white screen which had been built at one end of the experimenting room. So true to life were the figures, and so perfect was the reproduction of each motion that the spectator would almost believe that the girls were real and that the machine which clicked and sputtered had

nothing to do with the performance.

No one was more pleased at the success of his work than the great inventor himself. Wrapped in a big overcoat which hung to his knees and rose to his hat brim he walked about the cold room chuckling and joking with the men who had done so much to make his work what it is.

The figure of a girl dressed for a skirt dance was thrown upon the screen. The delicate colors of the shimmering silk were shown as distinctly as though a calcium light were being thrown upon a living dancer on a real stage. Mr. Edison . . . walked close to the screen to note more precisely the effect of the draperies and the flesh tints on the arms and face of the young woman. As the graceful figure showed now and then when the yards of silk were sent floating high in the air, Edison smiled. Then, as the dancer smiled and brushed away the locks of curling hair which had fallen over her eyes during the dance, the inventor clapped his hands, and . . . said: 'That is good enough to warrant our establishing a bald head row, and we will do it' " (*New York Journal*, 4 April 1896).

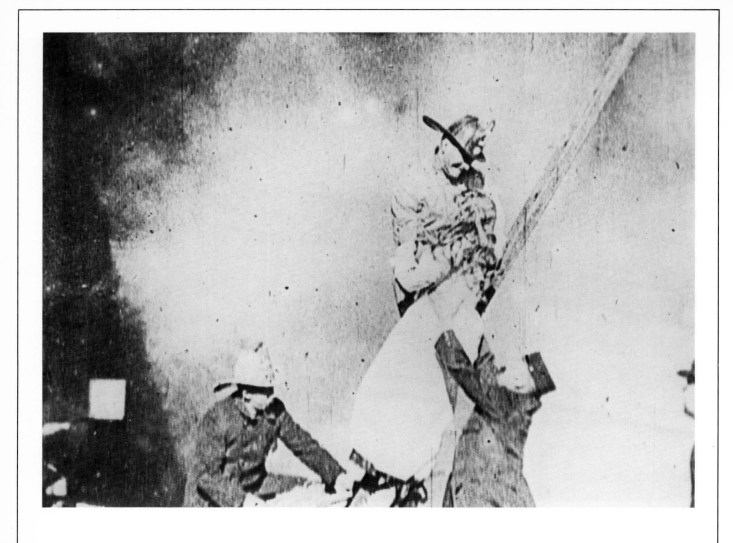

Fire Rescue

1894. Edison Manufacturing Company. Photographed by W.K.L. Dickson and William Heise.
Shot at Edison's Black Maria studio in West Orange, New Jersey, between 1 October and 17 December 1894.
Print source: George Eastman House. 27 sec.

The letter *R* in the left foreground of the frame indicates that it was shot for Raff and Gammon of the Kinetoscope Company, rather than for Maguire and Baucus, Edison's foreign agents. The symbol was not used before 1 October 1894. A still from *Fire Rescue* appears in the Dickson booklet, thus indicating that it was shot before 17 December. The elaborateness of the production, with smoke effects, costumes, and quite possibly the use of the Orange Fire Department, indicates a date toward the end of the period 1 October–17 December 1894. The original film can bears the title: "Fire Rescue—H & L" (Hook and Ladder).
—Gordon Hendricks

Shooting the Chutes

Premiered 29 June 1896. Edison Manufacturing Company. Photographed by William Heise.
Shot at Coney Island, New York. Print source: George Eastman House. 29 sec.

The popular diversion, "shoot-the-chutes," was built at Coney Island in 1895 by Captain Paul Boyton. It was widely illustrated in contemporary periodicals and was a favorite subject for amateur photographers. Two versions are listed in the Maguire and Baucus catalogue, one of 50 feet and the other of 150. We can understand the difference between them through the Asbury Park *Journal* of 5 August 1896: "[this subject] shows the long slide and the dash into the water with remarkable accuracy and life." Since the present subject shows only "the long slide" and not "the dash into the water," it is obvious that we have here the first part of the subject. According to the New York *Dramatic*

Mirror of 11 July 1896, it was projected by the Vitascope at Koster and Bial's the week beginning 29 June. This suggests a shooting date not later than 22 June.

—Gordon Hendricks

"The entire variety bill this week [at Keith's Theater] is exceptionally strong. The new views on the Vitascope—especially the shooting-the-chutes scene from the Battery, New York, and the suburban handicap race—are received at every performance with shouts of approval" (*Boston Herald* [14 July 1896], p. 6).

Market Square, Harrisburg, Pa.

© 8 January 1897. Edison Manufacturing Company. Photographed by James H. White and William Heise.
Shot in Harrisburg, Pennsylvania, on 24–26 December 1896. Print source: George Eastman House. 29 sec.

The camera stood approximately in the middle of Market Street, between Front and Second Street. Edison's projectorscope had been playing at the Bijou Theatre in Harrisburg since 23 November, and as was often the case in those eager days, it was thought that local views would add zest to the presentation. On 23 December cameramen from the Edison plant arrived in Harrisburg and began shooting. Seven subjects were copyrighted. Unfortunately the films were not finished before the projectorscope left Harrisburg and went on the road.   —Gordon Hendricks

The story continues. An exhibitor not associated with Bijou Theater manager Foley purchased the views from the Edison Company and suddenly opened them at Harrisburg's rival Grand Opera House on 13 and 14 January. Although Foley had paid to have the views taken and was planning to show them in his own theater in the near future, he was caught unprepared. He tried to block the exhibition with a court injunction but was unsuccessful. Although he showed the local views at his theater the following week, the manager only charged an admission fee of 5 cents and 10 cents—half what the Opera House received.   —C. M.

The Famous Views

"Harrisburg on the Projectoscope at the Grand Opera House. The sudden announcement that the much talked of Harrisburg views will be shown at the Grand Opera House, for four performances, commencing with a dime matinee, to-day has aroused the greatest interest and despite the short notice a large crowd promises to see the very first of the local pictures. It will be a strange and novel sight for our townsmen to see themselves pictured the same as in every day life and many a well-known personage will be easily recognized in the crowds that line the sidewalks and that participate in the various views which will be presented" (*Harrisburg Patriot* [13 January 1897], p. 2).

Railway Station Scene

February 1897. International Film Company. Photographed by Edmund Kuhn or Charles Webster.
Shot in Elizabeth, New Jersey. Print source: George Eastman House. 28 sec.

This film was shot in Elizabeth, New Jersey, immediately
to the west of the Pennsylvania Railroad tracks, by a
cameraman of the International Film Company, possibly
Edmund Kuhn. At the time the film was made there were
two intertrack barriers on the four-track Pennsylvania Railroad line. Late February 1897 appears an approximate date.
—Gordon Hendricks

The Passion Play of Oberammergau (Select Scenes)
"Salome's Dance" "The Messiah's Entry into Jerusalem" "The Ascension"

Premiered 30 January 1898. Eden Musée . Produced by Richard Hollaman and Albert Eaves. Directed by Henry C. Vincent.
Photographed by William Paley. With Frank Russell (Christ), Frank Gaylor (Judas Iscariot), Fred Strong (Pontius Pilate). Based on Salmi Morse's
adaptation of the *Passion Play* performed in Oberammergau, Bavaria. Shot on the rooftop of the Grand Central Palace, New York City,
December–January 1898. Print source: George Eastman House. 2 min.

Richard Hollaman's Eden Musée, an amusement center featuring waxworks and musical programs, was located on 23rd Street, then a fashionable New York entertainment district. Moving pictures were added to its programming on 18 December 1896, and late in 1897 Hollaman moved into film production with a subject that was reputed to reenact the famous Oberammergau *Passion Play* (in fact many of the scenes were not in the Bavarian spectacle). Twenty-three scenes—each a separate film—were photographed for a total running time of approximately 19 minutes. These, however, were only the raw material for a far more elaborate program. According to one trade journal, "A lecture accompanies the showing of the pictures and by the addition of lantern slides in keeping with the subject, an entertainment of two or so hours can be given" (*The Phonoscope* [March 1898], p. 7).

When Hollaman opened the film at the Eden Musée, it was even more favorably received than anticipated. One month after the Musée opening the *New York Mail and Express* reported, "The cinematograph pictures of the Passion Play are attracting thousands of people at the Eden Musée. . . . So many ministers and church people are present at both the afternoon and evening exhibitions of the pictures that the Musée seems much like a church . . ." (1 March 1898, p. 7).

In 1900 during the stage performances of the Oberammergau *Passion Play*, a New York-based cameraman filmed four different scenes of events surrounding the play's presentation. These and the twenty-three original films, which Edison also acquired for its catalogue, were sold individually enabling exhibitors to select a program that fit their purposes and pocketbook. Exhibitions of the *Passion Play of Oberammergau* differed in length, order, narration, and format.

—C. M.

The Battle of Manila Bay

May 1898. American Vitagraph Company. Distributed by Edison Manufacturing Company. Produced by J. Stuart Blackton and Albert E. Smith.
Shot on the rooftop of Vitagraph's headquarters at 140 Nassau Street, New York City, ca. 19 May 1898. Print source: George Eastman House.
33 sec.

Blackton and Smith began to make their own films in May 1898. These were intended for their own exclusive use, providing their exhibitors with special subjects that no other showman could offer. Soon the partners were sued by Thomas Edison for infringement on his motion picture patents. Rather than contest the suit, the duo became Edison licensees. As part of this arrangement, Edison marketed their films to exhibitors and gave Blackton and Smith a royalty of 30 cents for each 50-foot print that was sold. Edison often copyrighted their subjects in his own name to prevent illegal duplication. As a result, many of these films have been falsely attributed to Edison personnel.

Later in life, Albert Smith remembered the making of *Battle of Manila Bay*: "At this time street vendors in New York City were selling sturdy photographs of ships of the American and Spanish fleets. We bought a set of each and we cut out the battleships. On a table, topside down, we placed one of artist Blackton's large canvas-covered frames and filled it with water an inch deep. In order to stand the cutouts in the water, we nailed them to lengths of wood about an inch square. In this way a little "shelf" was provided behind each ship and on this shelf we placed pinches of gunpowder—three pinches for each ship—not too many, we felt, for a major sea engagement of this sort" (Albert E. Smith with Phil A. Koury, *Two Reels and a Crank* [Garden City, N.Y.: Doubleday, 1952], pp. 66–67). —C.M.

Soldiers at Play

Premiered 16 May 1898. William Selig. Shot at Camp Tanner,
Springfield, Illinois, during early May. Print source: George Eastman House.
26 sec.

The Spanish-American War encouraged Chicago-based exhibitor William Selig to move into production too. His camera crew traveled to Camp Tanner in Springfield, Illinois, where most of the state's volunteers were being trained. During this trip they filmed the troops parading past the Governor's mansion as well as scenes of camp life such as this one. Less than a week later, these scenes were being shown at Chicago's Schiller Theater between acts of the opera *The Beggar Student*. According to the *Chicago Inter-Ocean*, "A feature which caught the crowds was the presentation of a series of cinematograph pictures representing scenes of camp life at Camp Tanner. They showed the Illinois volunteers at the various camp avocations: drilling, parading, on review and at their sports. All the pictures are good and they were cheered to the echo. They will remain a feature during the entire week" (*Chicago Inter-Ocean*, 17 May 1898, p. 6). —C. M.

Raising Old Glory Over Morro Castle

© 4 February 1899. American Vitagraph Company. Distributed by Edison Manufacturing Company. Produced by J. Stuart Blackton and Albert E. Smith. Set design by J. Stuart Blackton. Shot at Vitagraph's rooftop studio at 140 Nassau Street, New York City. Print source: Library of Congress. 41 sec.

The rise of the motion picture coincided with a crucial phase in American history during which the United States made its debut as a colonial power with overseas possessions. There was some opposition to America's new role: the Anti-Imperialist League was formed, and William Jennings Bryan was about to run for President on an anti-imperialist platform. Even so, the prevailing mood of the country was more muscular and exhilarated, and the two developments—cinema and imperialism—fanned each other. A simple shot, such as the pulling down of a Spanish flag and raising of an American one in its place, could send audiences into ecstasies. Actualities of events in Cuba, the arrival and departure of troops, men drilling, reenactments of naval battles such as Admiral Dewey's victory at Manila Bay, all drew crowds to theaters.

—Erik Barnouw

"Havana. Jan. 1. Spain's historical flag floats no longer in the Antilles. The Stars and Stripes went up at noon to-day with impressive simplicity. The ceremony which sealed the yielding of Spanish sovereignty in Cuba took place in the Palace. The mass of the population could not be admitted there and the people of Havana gathered along the Punta, at the foot of the Prado and opposite Morro Castle and Cabanas Fortress. They saw the Spanish colors go up on Morro and receive the salutes of guns from Cabanas and from the American warships in the harbor. Quickly they saw the yellow and red standard come down and the American flag floating over Morro, Cabanas and the other forts of the city, while they heard the salute in its honor from the Spanish artillery which has been kept in Cabanas for that purpose, and also from the Spanish ships which were remaining in the harbor" (*New York Tribune* [2 January 1899], p. 1)

Blackton Sketching Edison

1896. Edison Manufacturing Company. Photographed by William Heise. With J. Stuart Blackton. Probably shot at Raff and Gammon's makeshift rooftop studio on West 28th Street, New York City, in July or early August 1896. Print source: Museum of Modern Art. 1.5 min.

J. Stuart Blackton, a young cartoonist with the *New York World*, and Albert E. Smith, his partner in Lyceum entertainments, donated their services to the *World*'s Sick Baby Fund during the summer of 1896 in exchange for publicity and newspaper reviews. On one occasion, Blackton was filmed performing three lightning sketches, causing the Vitascope Company to donate $25 to the Sick Baby Fund. When the vitascope played at F. F. Proctor's two New York vaudeville theaters in September 1896, the film of Blackton sketching Edison was featured on both bills. According to the *Mail and Express*, "The most curious and interesting of the new views was that showing the rapid sketching of the Wizard Edison's portrait by a well-known cartoonist. Every stroke of the crayon was reproduced until the excellent likeness was perfected" (*New York Mail and Express*, 15 September 1896, p. 5).   —C. M.

J. Stuart Blackton's 1896 sketch of Thomas A. Edison for the *New York Evening World*, which provided the inspiration for the film *Blackton Sketching Edison* of the same year.

Burglar on the Roof

1898. American Vitagraph Company. Distributed by Edison Manufacturing Company. Photographed by Albert E. Smith. With J. Stuart Blackton as the burglar, Mrs. Olsen (wife of building superintendent), Vitagraph employees and friends (including Charles Urban). Shot at Vitagraph's rooftop studio in September 1898. Print source: George Eastman House. 2 min.

Impressed by moving pictures, Blackton and Smith bought an Edison projector and some films in February 1897 and became motion picture exhibitors. In May 1898, they converted a projector into a camera and began to make their own films. Calling themselves the American Vitagraph Company, the duo made *Burglar on the Roof* using friends and employees. The film was indebted to simple newspaper comics which had a much larger audience. The burglar was a popular cartoon character ("Burglar Bill," "Happy Hooligan" and many others) whose unsuccessful robberies usually resulted in some kind of amusing punishment. The comedy was being shown at Proctor's Pleasure Palace by early October and was a favorite selection for many years.

—C. M.

A Visit to the Spiritualist

1899. American Vitagraph Company. Photographed by Albert E. Smith and J. Stuart Blackton. Shot at Vitagraph's rooftop studio in late 1899. Print source: UCLA Film Archives. 2 min.

Vitagraph's growing resources and expertise are evident in *A Visit to the Spiritualist*. While Frenchman Georges Méliès was considered the master of the trick film, Albert Smith's training and continued activities as a magician made him a capable producer of such films, too. According to one distributor, the subject "is acknowledged by the exhibitors to be the funniest of all moving picture magical films" (Edison Manufacturing Company, *Edison Films* [March 1900], p. 40). The spiritualist's power, which overwhelms the country rube who comes to visit, is really the power of technology which Blackton and Smith had mastered and which urban audiences appreciated at the rube's expense.

—C. M.

The Tramp's Dream

1899. Sigmund Lubin. Produced by John F. Frawley and Jacob Blair Smith (?). Shot at Lubin's rooftop studio at 912 Arch Street, Philadelphia, in the fall of 1899. Print source: George Eastman House. 1.5 min.

Although Lubin's productions have often been dismissed by film historians because of his tendency to imitate other people's productions, *The Tramp's Dream* suggests this attitude is unjustified. Multiple-shot films such as this one were still very unusual in 1899. When they were made, dreams or subjective viewpoints often provided the links between different scenes. This three-shot comedy, listed by a Lubin sales agent in November 1899, was imitated by rival producers. In 1901, Edwin Porter of the Edison Company made a very similar film with the same title and Biograph's *Hooligan's Christmas Dream*, made in late 1903, was likewise similar.

—C. M.

Searching Ruins on Broadway, Galveston, for Dead Bodies

© 24 September 1900. American Vitagraph Company. Produced by J. Stuart Blackton and Albert E. Smith. Distributed by Edison Manufacturing Company. Shot on location in Galveston, Texas. Print source: Library of Congress. 50 sec.

Film people, then as now, were drawn to disasters. If they could not be on the spot, they were willing to re-create reality with table-top animation, as did Billy Bitzer for films of the San Francisco earthquake and Vesuvius eruption. But this film on the effects of the Galveston hurricane is exactly what it appears to be. *Searching Ruins on Broadway, Galveston, for Dead Bodies* itself was resurrected from the rubble of

history, having survived solely as a paper print deposited for copyright.
—Erik Barnouw

"The vitagraph shows views taken on the spot at Galveston, Texas, immediately after the great disaster by flood, and the pictures are graphic enough to help swell the relief fund" (*Boston Herald*, 25 September 1900, p. 9).

Scenes of the Wreckage from the Waterfront

September 1900. Sigmund Lubin. Photographed by J. Blair Smith (?). Shot at Galveston, Texas, in September 1900. Print source: George Eastman House. 1.5 min.

"Lubin's Operators the First on the Scene" (Lubin advertisement, *New York Clipper* [29 September 1900], p. 696).

Beheading the Chinese Prisoner

1900. Sigmund Lubin. Produced by John F. Frawley and Jacob Blair Smith (?). Shot at Lubin's rooftop studio at
912 Arch Street, Philadelphia, in July or early August 1900. Print source: George Eastman House. 42 sec.

Hoping to cash in on the so-called "Boxer Rebellion," the Lubin Company released a series of films in the summer of 1900, including *Chinese Massacring Christians* (sic), *In the Pillory, Bombarding and Capturing the Taku Forts,* and this film. A contemporary advertisement and the 1903 Lubin catalogue indicate that the producers sold *Beheading the Chinese Prisoner* as a "just received" film document straight from the raging war:

"A Chinese prisoner is tried before one of the chiefs, and being found guilty, is sentenced to be beheaded, which sentence is immediately executed. The executioner displays the head to the spectators to serve as a warning for evil doers. Very exciting." (S. Lubin, *Complete Catalogue, Lubin's Films* [January 1903], p. 54).

In fact, this film was shot at the Lubin studio, since it and *Chinese Massacring Christians* display painted backdrops and an identical papier-mâché chopping block. Also, the exclusively Caucasian actors are dressed in traditional Chinese, rather than modern, dress, thus reinforcing contemporary stereotypes.   —Jan-Christopher Horak

How They Rob Men in Chicago

1900. American Mutoscope and Biograph Company. Produced by Wallace McCutcheon. Photographed by Arthur Marvin. Shot at Biograph's rooftop studio at 841 Broadway, New York City, on 24 April 1900. Print source: American Film Institute. 23 sec.

Until 1902, Biograph shot all of its films using a large-format 70mm stock. Films were also shot at about 30 frames per second as opposed to approximately 18 to 20 for most 35mm producers. The result was a superior image, even though the Biograph camera used six times as much film for the same amount of screen time as a 35mm camera. Perhaps because raw stock was expensive, early Biograph comedies were often quite short. Later, Biograph used an optical printing process to make 35mm films from these negatives and, in at least some cases, copied only alternate frames, reducing the number of frames per second.

Under the alternate title of *How They Entertain Strangers in Chicago*, Biograph offered the following description of this film:

"A burlesque on the work of highwaymen in Chicago. An elderly gentleman is sandbagged and robbed by a thug, who inadvertently leaves some money on the victim's prostrate body. A policeman happening along, takes the money and passes by without paying any attention to the plight of the victim" (American Mutoscope & Biograph Company, *Picture Catalogue* [November 1902], p. 33). —C. M.

An Unexpected Knockout

June 1901. American Mutoscope and Biograph Company. Produced by Wallace McCutcheon. Photographed by Frederick S. Armitage.
Shot at Biograph's rooftop studio on 7 June 1901. Print source: American Film Institute. 23 sec.

"Two Boys are fighting over a game. An inquisitive old gentleman interferes and urges them on. One seizes a bag of flour and attempts to strike the other. The intended victim ducks, and the old gentleman gets the contents of the bag" (American Mutoscope & Biograph Company, *Picture Catalogue* [November 1902], p. 46).

He Forgot His Umbrella

June 1901. American Mutoscope and Biograph Company. Produced by Wallace McCutcheon. Photographed by Frederick S. Armitage. Shot at Biograph's rooftop studio on 29 June 1901. Print source: American Film Institute. 19 sec.

Infidelity and illicit relationships were the frequent subjects of early Biograph films. This frequency suggests a preoccupation that was social as well as psychological. Life in the large, impersonal cities made extramarital affairs more possible, and a source of heightened anxiety for many who had recently moved from the countryside where communities were more closely knit.

The Biograph company's all-male production team seemed to find compromising situations to be the source of endless merriment, as in this short comedy. "A gay old gentleman dining with a pretty girl in a private dining room, leaves for a short time but forgets his umbrella as he goes out. In the meantime a young man enters and proceeds to take the old boy's place," is how Biograph's publicist introduced *He Forgot His Umbrella*. Private dining rooms were favorite places for discreet rendezvous, and this elderly gentleman is undoubtedly meeting his mistress. Although the old man is seemingly outwitted by the woman's lover, the tables are quickly turned by his unexpected return.

—C. M.

A Mighty Tumble

November 1901. American Mutoscope and Biograph Company. Photographed by James Congdon. Shot on Jackson Avenue
in Jersey City, New Jersey, in early November 1901. Print source: Museum of Modern Art. 17 sec.

Production companies were very casual when naming
their films and sometimes gave them three or even four
different titles. To further complicate the problem of identification, films were often renamed by the exhibitors who
purchased them. Biograph catalogues labeled this view both
A Mighty Tumble and *The Fall of a Brick Building*. One title
was colorful and catchy while the other literally described
the subject. In this way, the same film might appeal to
different customers.　　　　　　　　　　　　　　—C. M.

"Razing a four story brick building. The structure is pushed
over as a whole and falls with a terrific crash. The picture is
very effective and unusual" (American Mutoscope and Biograph Company, *Picture Catalogue* [November 1902],
p. 247).

Next!

1903. American Mutoscope and Biograph Company. Produced by Wallace McCutcheon and Frank Marion (?). Photographed by A. E. Weed. Shot at Biograph's indoor electric light studio at 11 East 14th Street, New York City, on 4 November 1903. Print source: Library of Congress. 1 min.

Biograph, in particular, made free use of popular cartoon characters in its comedies: Happy Hooligan, Burglar Bill, Foxy Grandpa, Mr. Butt-in and others. Among this group were Alphonse and Gaston, the creations of Frederick Burr Opper, who were used for several short comedies. *Next!* was shot using 35mm stock and made in Biograph's new electric light studio, the first of its kind in the world. Using Cooper-Hewitt lights, filming could go on rain or shine, day or night.

As multi-shot films became more common, filmmakers were increasingly concerned with creating a spatial/temporal world through the juxtaposition of shots. Biograph—like the Edison Company before it—followed the lead of Georges Méliès whose influential *A Trip to the Moon* (1902) showed a rocket hitting the Man in the Moon at the end of one shot and then landing on the moon at the beginning of the next one. In *Next!*, the moment when the two characters are thrown through the window is the obvious high point of the film. By showing the event from two different perspectives (inside and outside), spectators could have the pleasure of seeing the window-shattering crash twice. —C. M.

Smashing a Jersey Mosquito

1902. Edison Manufacturing Company. Produced and photographed by Edwin S. Porter. Shot at Edison's 21st Street studio, New York City, during the summer or fall of 1902. Print source: American Film Institute. 50 sec.

In an earlier film, *A Jersey Skeeter* (Biograph, 1900), a huge mosquito attacks a New Jersey farmer, seizes him by the seat of his pants and carries him away. In this Edison film, a man is able to defend himself and his wife somewhat more effectively.

—C. M.

The Burning of Durland's Riding Academy

© 24 February 1902. Edison Manufacturing Company. Photographed by Jacob Blair Smith or Edwin S. Porter. Shot between Broadway and Central Park West, 61st and 62nd Streets, New York City, on 15 February 1902. Print source: American Film Institute. 2 min.

The film's sweeping panoramas suggest the ease with which motion picture photographers adjusted their camera frame when filming news events, scenery and other actualities. This was still not the case with staged scenes using actors. Even when the setting for fictional films was outside, as in *Capture of the Biddle Brothers* (Edison, February 1902), the Edison camera was consistently static. Only late in 1902 did Porter begin to use camera movement to follow staged action, and only then with exterior scenes. The breakdown of this dichotomy was a lengthy process that took many years.

By the time Edison offered this film for sale, it was retitled *Firemen Fighting the Flames at Paterson* and attributed to a larger, more important fire that had taken place in Paterson, New Jersey, on 9 February. Edison cameramen had filmed the devastation resulting from that fire but not the fire itself. Audiences expecting a film of actual firefighting were given the "Durland" film with the misleading "Paterson" title. —C. M.

Electrocuting an Elephant

© 12 January 1903. Edison Manufacturing Company. Photographed by Jacob Blair Smith or Edwin S. Porter.
Shot at Luna Park, Coney Island, on 4 January 1903. Print source: Library of Congress. 1 min.

"While fifteen hundred persons looked on in breathless excitement, an electric bolt of 6,000 volts sent Topsy, the man-killing elephant, staggering to the ground yesterday afternoon at Luna Park, Coney Island. With her own life [she] paid for the lives of the three men she had killed.

"It was all over in a moment. Wooden sandals containing the deadly electrodes had been fitted to Topsy's feet; wires from the shoe on the right fore foot and from that on the left hind foot made the connection for the shock; the current was turned on in a house a hundred feet away, and quick as a flash the colossal form of the elephant stiffened forward, then quivered in the throes of the mighty bolt, sinking finally to the ground without a groan . . .

". . . Topsy was the original 'Baby Elephant.' She was brought to this country by Adam Forepaugh twenty-eight years ago. She was then eight years old. She weighed at the time of her death four tons, and she was worth $4,000 . . .

". . . Joseph Johansen, the electrician in charge of the Edison electric-light station, narrowly escaped death in turning the switches that threw the entire voltage into the wire that was to carry death to Topsy. As he threw the last switch he got the full force of the current through his arm and down his right side to the calf of his leg" (*New York World* [5 January 1903], pp. 1–2).

What Happened on Twenty-Third Street, New York City

© 21 August 1901. Edison Manufacturing Company. Photographed by Edwin S. Porter. With Alfred C. Abadie and Florence Georgie. Shot in Herald Square, 23rd Street, New York City. Print source: Library of Congress. 1 min.

This primitive bit of early film catches a young woman in a light summer dress approaching a grate-covered manhole on a pavement. As the woman steps on the grate, escaping air from below blows her dress upward above her knees to reveal her undergarments.

In the infant movie trade of that day, similar embarrassing scenes were staged and included in film programs. They were called "Teasers," a carry-over from the peep-show cabinets and kinetoscope machines of the Penny Arcades. Such teasers were supposed to add spice and entertainment to film programs commonly made up of more conservative subjects such as views, news items, skits, and song slides.

—Lewis Jacobs

Trapeze Disrobing Act

© 11 November 1901. Edison Manufacturing Company. Produced and photographed by Edwin S. Porter.
Shot at Edison's 21st Street studio. Print source: American Film Institute. 1 min.

This film of a fully clothed trapeze artist suspended on a bar in midair above a stage demonstrated her skill on the high bar as well as her adroitness in undressing. By the film's end—less than a minute later—the performer has completely disrobed except for a leotard.

Derived from vaudeville and burlesque routines, the picture not only satisfied the lust of the eye, but also added a sense of suspense to the action. Both qualities were to play increasing roles in the development of the medium's technique and economic growth. —Lewis Jacobs

What Happened in the Tunnel

© 6 November 1903. Edison Manufacturing Company. Photographed by Edwin S. Porter. With Gilbert M. Anderson.
Shot in Fort Lee, New Jersey, and Edison's 21st Street studio, on 30 and 31 October 1903. Print source: Library of Congress. 1 min.

What Happened in the Tunnel takes place on the set of a moving train. A young man retrieves a handkerchief dropped by a young girl seated with her maid. As the man returns the kerchief to its owner, he attempts to kiss her. At that moment the train enters a darkened tunnel, and the screen blacks out. When the train emerges from the tunnel, the man is horrified to discover that he is embracing the maid, who is black. Even during these early stages of movie making, the screen was beginning to reflect some of the social attitudes and ideas of the day.

In an earlier film, *The Life of an American Fireman* (Edison, 1902–3), Porter combined staged and unstaged shots, but here he stages the entire film, basing it on the theatrical device of a blackout, with its narrative logic of beginning, middle, and end. In this regard, the tunnel picture can be seen as a transitional work leading to Porter's next picture, *The Great Train Robbery* (Edison, 1903), made with more elaborate material, greater narrative construction, and a unique cinematic form that revolutionized film production. —Lewis Jacobs

The Story the Biograph Told

© 8 January 1904. American Mutoscope and Biograph Company. Produced by Wallace McCutcheon. Photographed by A. E. Weed. Shot at Biograph's 14th Street studio, New York City, 30 November 1903. Print source: Library of Congress. 3 min.

As in a number of early films, the motion picture apparatus plays a major role in this Biograph comedy. The film uses a situation common to short stories and popular mythology from this period: a presumably private infraction of propriety becomes inadvertently public through the intervention of the motion picture camera. This plot was conceivable only during the first decades of the cinema when bits of everyday life, rather than fictional dramas, made up the greater part of film programs. Film became a new way of mixing the realms of private and public life, in this case revealing things normally concealed and causing social embarrassment. The agent of embarrassing revelation is a familiar figure in early film, the mischievous boy, who uses film to carry out his practical joke.

The film within the film is projected in a vaudeville theater as one act among others on the bill (the cards announcing the name of the acts are shown). During this period vaudeville theaters were the most frequent places of exhibition for films, as Biograph acknowledges by this setting. Two filmings of a single action are shown, although separated in time. In one, the straight-on view of the philandering husband and secretary is seen, and in the other, a later side view from a closer position as filmed by the office boy is presented. The idea of point-of-view editing is indicated, if somewhat ambiguously, by cutting directly from a view of the theater and audience to the film shown on the screen. Finally and most curiously, the idea of simultaneity is expressed through superimposing two shots rather than intercutting them. While ". . . the office boy seizes the opportunity to make a moving picture of the love scene, . . . the proprietor's wife calls him up on the 'phone, and by a dissolving effect the wife is shown at the 'phone while the husband with the girl in his lap is talking at the other end, the small boy in the meantime grinding away at the camera" (Biograph publicity bulletin, 1905). This ingenious solution to the problem of presenting simultaneous events produces a rather complicated image, and is the only example I know of its use. A split screen was the usual solution, but by 1908 similar situations would begin to be handled by crosscutting.

—Tom Gunning

Pull Down the Curtains, Suzie

© 12 January 1904. American Mutoscope and Biograph Company. Produced by Wallace McCutcheon. Photographed by A. E. Weed. Shot at Biograph's 14th Street studio, New York City, on 30 December 1903. Print source: Library of Congress. 39 sec.

Produced by the American Mutoscope and Biograph Company for use in their mutoscope viewer (a peep-show device that used a series of flipped cards), this one-shot film may never have been shown as such, probably because of its slightly scandalous nature. However, very similar films were projected at the time, and, while this film may be titillating, it is, as film scholar Jay Leyda once called it, "baby blue" compared to other erotic films from the period that often included full nudity.

Many early films and peep-show productions followed the same brief format; a single incident is presented, and, once its immediate attraction is exhausted, the film ends. In

Pull Down the Curtains, Suzie the attraction is an explicit erotic voyeurism as a man watches a woman undressing in a window. However, full satisfaction is frustrated, as the title indicates, by a form of self-censorship in which Suzie pulls down the window shade before removing her undergarments. One of many examples of the erotic display of scantily dressed women in early cinema, this film offers a man on the street who stands in for the film viewer. Through the rather unusual composition and set design of the film, the idea of a point of view is conveyed in a single shot.

—Tom Gunning

Meet Me at the Fountain

© 19 November 1904. Sigmund Lubin. Cast features female impersonator Gilbert Saroni as the Successful Woman.
Shot in Philadelphia during the fall of 1904. Print source: American Film Institute. 4 min.

As it survives, *Meet Me at the Fountain* is a baffling early chase comedy, with malicious women chasing an apparently innocent dandy. Originally, the situation must have been evident through an opening title along the lines of the "personals" advertisement printed in Lubin's own film ad: "A French Nobleman, recently arrived in America, desires to meet a handsome American girl. Object matrimony. Will be AT THE FOUNTAIN at 10 A.M. wearing a Chrysanthemum as Boutonniere" (*New York Clipper* [5 November 1904]).

Lubin's was at least the second plagiarism, almost shot for shot, of a successful Biograph comedy, *Personal*, filmed in June 1904. Edison's entry, in August, was self-explanatorily titled *How a French Nobleman Got a Wife Through the New York Herald Personal Column*. The original title for Lubin's brazen remake was *A New Version of "Personal."* Remarkably, all survive. This Lubin version is distinctive for its early use of lap dissolves to join each shot, making the film strange to today's audiences grown accustomed to that bit of film grammar as signifying a leap in time and space.

—Scott Simmon

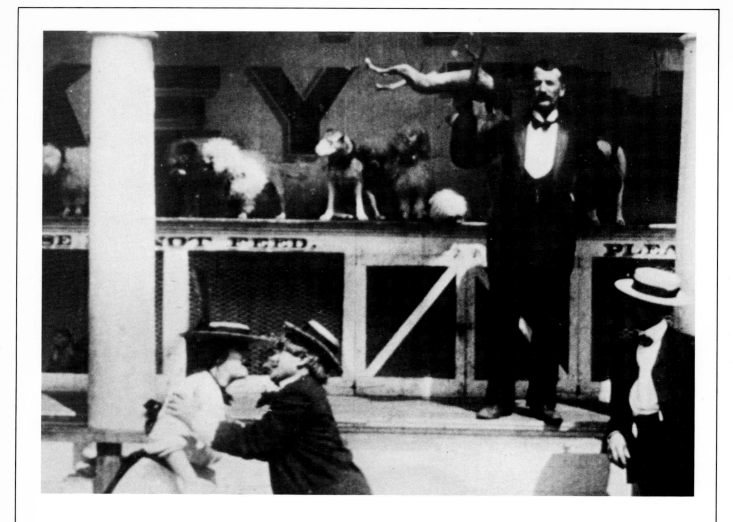

Rube and Mandy at Coney Island

© 13 August 1903. Edison Manufacturing Company. Produced and photographed by Edwin S. Porter. Shot at Coney Island and at Edison's 21st Street studio, New York City, in early August 1903. Print source: Museum of Modern Art. 10 min.

This is a comedy in which two leading vaudeville performers play country bumpkins taking in the wonders of Coney Island in 1903. It is a series of comic episodes connected by a common motif rather than an integrated narrative. It demonstrates how early cinema employed close views as a coda to the main structure of a film, with its final shot of Rube and Mandy enjoying hot dogs.

—Eileen Bowser

"The children do enjoy the journey of Mandy and Reuben to Coney Island as shown in the electrograph. It is worth bringing them to see. It was a hit last night even with the grown-ups. Loop the loop, shoot the chutes. Mandy and Rube took it all in. Their journey is accurately followed in the motion picture" (*New Haven Journal-Courier*, 3 September 1903, p 6).

The European Rest Cure

July 1904. Edison Manufacturing Company. Produced and photographed by Edwin S. Porter. Shot at Edison's 21st Street studio, New York City, and New York area. Print source: Museum of Modern Art/Library of Congress. 11 min.

An elderly businessman packed off to Europe for a relaxing holiday returns home a battered wreck.

The film's elaborate departure sequence includes scenes photographed at the New York City docks as well as three pieces of Edison company "actuality" footage—*S.S.* Coptic *Running Against the Storm* (1898) and *Pilot Leaving* Prinzessin Victoria Luise *at Sandy Hook* (1902), both taken by James White, and *Skyscrapers of New York from the North River* (1903), taken by Jacob Blair Smith. Mélièsian studio tableaux, which incorporate trick effects and stop-motion photography, depict the seasick traveler and his unhappy experiences in Ireland, France, Switzerland, Italy, Egypt, and Germany.

It is not clear whether Porter was aiming his satirical hose at inept Americans abroad or the perceived menace of travel in Europe. The roughhouse treatment of European scenes had its roots in the broad ethnic comedy common to vaudeville amusements of the period. The apparent xenophobia that located Egypt in Europe really ought to be considered in the context of the huge success enjoyed by motion pictures that dealt with travel and foreign places.

—David Levy

The Strenuous Life, or, Anti-Race Suicide

1904. Edison Manufacturing Company. Produced and photographed by Edwin S. Porter. With Kathryn Osterman. Shot at Edison's
21st Street studio, New York City, and on Manhattan streets, 8, 9, 14 December 1904. Print source: Museum of Modern Art. 4 min.

The Strenuous Life is paradigmatic. It was shot flat-on at what had become conventional camera distance, that is, theatrical front-row center. The film tends toward an elegant and pointed manner of storytelling in its second scene in which the camera tracks the development of plot and provides a little suspense as the businessman from scene one fetches a doctor to go home with him in scene three. The second scene also illustrates the serendipity of shooting exteriors on a New York City street—passers-by and an elevated railway make unrehearsed appearances.

A startling punctuation occurs in the fourth and final scene in which the narrative, interrupted by a closer view of the action, repeats in half figure the scene already played at a greater distance in full figure. However, most of the narrative gist of the comedy occurs *after* this shot, with the camera back at its standard, less-intimate distance. The businessman, having been given one baby, is delivered three more infants. Holding two of his issue, he faints into a chair, is revived, and in response to the multiple births boots the doctor out of the room. While the two serving women are consternated—playing both to each other and to the camera—the father, resigned to his quadruplets, once more collapses into his chair. The tight shot with its detailed view of smiling father and housekeeper weighing a baby refreshes the narrative and has a pleasant emotional effect, but its potential to develop the story is unrealized. The effective narrative strategy would be to use the shot much as the punch line to a joke (for the father's collapse or the unanticipated aggression toward the doctor), and not for replay, but this had yet to be learned. *The Strenuous Life* is charming proof that narrative style is not self-evident, natural, or irresistible. —Laurence Kardish

This film lightheartedly spoofs Theodore Roosevelt who had just been re-elected President. He believed Americans had to lead "the strenuous life" if the United States was to retain its position of world leadership. He also felt that married women of northern European stock had a responsibility to produce at least four children to prevent "race-suicide." —C.M.

The Suburbanite

© 11 November 1904. American Mutoscope and Biograph Company. Directed by Wallace McCutcheon, Sr. Scenario by Frank Marion and/or Wallace McCutcheon, Sr. Photographed by A. E. Weed. With John Trioana, and possibly the children of Wallace McCutcheon, Sr., in support. Shot at the Biograph's 14th Street studio, New York City, and Asbury Park, New Jersey, on 21 and 22 October 1904. Print source: Museum of Modern Art/Library of Congress. 8 min.

Traveling to different locations outside New York City to film exterior scenes was part of the established routine for Biograph players and technicians by the time this film was made. The practice gave filmmakers first-hand experience of the tedium of commuting and provided the background for this film.

Among the places frequently chosen for exteriors were various middle-class communities along the New Jersey coast. All of these towns were served by the New Jersey Central Railroad, which promoted its passenger services through a monthly magazine called *The Suburbanite*. This publication was freely distributed in waiting rooms and on commuter trains, and each issue was filled with breezy articles extolling suburban life over the crowded, expensive, and unhealthy conditions of apartment life in Manhattan.

This film was probably intended as a satire on both the magazine and suburban life in general. The intertitles, such as "A Sweet Little Home in the Country, Such a Nice Place for the Children," and "Within Easy Reach of the City," are among the first ever to appear in a Biograph comedy. Not only do these titles lampoon typical articles that appeared in *The Suburbanite*, they effectively form a counterpoint to the "realities" of the suburban experience depicted in the film's comic vignettes.

—Patrick G. Loughney

Program 2: Pleasures and Pitfalls

Photographing a Female Crook (1904).

Interior N. Y. Subway, 14th Street to 42nd Street

© 5 June 1905. American Mutoscope and Biograph Company. Photographed by G. W. Bitzer. Shot in Interborough Subway between 14th Street and 42nd Street, New York City, on 21 May 1905. Print source: Museum of Modern Art. 5 min.

One success of early cinema was Hale's Tours, an ingenious idea introduced at a Kansas City amusement park in 1905. A constructed railway carriage was entered by paying customers who saw a film that had been shot from the front of a moving train. The effect was sensational, but of greater historical and expressive importance were the endless series of variations on this idea: each of the followers brought more imagination to the idea than was brought by its inventor, Mr. Hale. *Interior N.Y. Subway* gives some impression of the swift current for inventiveness and surprise that kept nickelodeon spectators coming back for more.

—Jay Leyda

This film, while copyrighted separately, was usually sold as part of the Biograph comedy *Reuben in the Subway*.

—C. M.

Coney Island at Night

© 29 June 1905. Edison Manufacturing Company. Photographed by Edwin S. Porter. Title animation by Edwin S. Porter. Exterior scenes shot at Coney Island, New York, 3–4 June 1905. Print source: Museum of Modern Art/Library of Congress. 3 min.

In March 1905, Porter introduced a technique of title animation which he called "jumble announcements." Letters or cutouts were moved around a black background to spell words and form shapes. Porter used this innovation principally with comedies such as *How Jones Lost His Roll* (1905) and *The Whole Damm Family and The Damm Dog* (1905). *Coney Island at Night* was the only time that the filmmaker employed jumble announcements for an actuality subject. The stunning night photography was so effective that Porter subsequently reworked these scenes into *Tales the Searchlight Told* (Edison, 1908).   —C. M.

The Hold-up of the Rocky Mountain Express

© 12 April 1906. American Mutoscope and Biograph Company. Produced by Frank Marion.
Photographed by G. W. Bitzer. Shot in Phoenicia, New York on the Ulster and Delaware Railroad and at Biograph's 14th Street studio,
New York City, on 4–6 April 1906. Print source: Museum of Modern Art. 6 min.

This film was a rigorous application of the viewer-as-passenger convention which had been established in travelogues and similar turn-of-the-century entertainment. Since the 1890s many films had been taken from the front end of trains going through dramatic mountain scenery. Gradually this popular genre became more complex with the exhibitor inserting short comedies like *What Happened in the Tunnel* (Edison, 1903) into the scenic views. Although several train robbery films had been made by 1906, this was the only one that was specifically designed to be shown in a Hale's Tour Car, a specialized kind of picture theater that thrived in amusement parks during the summer of 1906. The car was designed to look like a railway carriage, both inside and out. Not only were the theaters designed to sway like a real train but the sound of wheels clattering on the rails was also added. The screen was at the front as if the spectators/travelers were looking out the front of an observation car. Films were usually shown via rear screen projection. In this context, *The Hold-up of the Rocky Mountain Express* was a hit, playing at the Brady-Grossman Hale's Tour near Union Square, New York City, for more than five weeks.

—C. M.

The Miller's Daughter

© 25 October 1905. Edison Manufacturing Company. Directed by Edwin S. Porter and Wallace McCutcheon. Produced and photographed by Edwin S. Porter. Filmed at Edison's 21st Street studio, New York City, and Scarsdale, New York, in September 1905. Print source: Museum of Modern Art. 11 min.

This sixteen-shot film is the fruit of an ambitious narrative project that needed some verbal explanations, probably given at each showing by an on-stage lecturer; without this, the film would have remained only partly understood.

The story is about Hazel, a young woman who is betrothed but chooses instead to elope with an artist. To Hazel's amazement, just as the minister is about to pronounce the couple man and wife, the artist's wife arrives and stops the illegal wedding. Hazel returns home but is banished by her infuriated father. She is so miserable that she throws herself into the rushing waters of a river in a suicide attempt. Luckily, the young farmer, her former lover, hears her screams of despair and saves her. They marry. Two years later, Hazel, with her husband and child, visits her father and is reconciled with him.

The story is told through a form of contrast structure recalling Porter's earlier film *The Kleptomaniac* (Edison, 1905). In *The Miller's Daughter*, alternating scenes show Hazel first with her artist-lover (shots one, three, and five) and then with the young farmer (shots two and four). The film also demonstrates several technical peculiarities. At least one shot has been enhanced with coloring effects (shot six). Horizontal pans in shot seven follow the characters; Hazel's vision of her father is superimposed in a circular matte; intertitles (one of which covers an ellipsis of two years) are used; and finally, the last shot contains a ceiling (probably painted on a drop) in a constructed set, which was quite unusual for the time.

—André Gaudreault

"The story is sweetly told, as a romance, and the ultimate happiness finds its place, when the will of the hard-hearted parent relents, and forgives his daughter for her rash act" (*Lewistown Evening Journal* [12 July 1907], p. 2).

The Miller's Daughter is a fascinating reworking of Steele MacKaye's stage play *Hazel Kirke* (1880) which was first performed at the Madison Square Theatre on 4 February 1880. After 486 performances, the play went on to become a standard number in the melodrama repertoire of various traveling theatrical troupes.

—C. M.

Getting Evidence

© 8 October 1906. Edison Manufacturing Company. Produced by Edwin S. Porter and Wallace McCutcheon. Photographed by Edwin S. Porter. Shot in the New York area on 20–24 September 1906. Print source: Museum of Modern Art. 10.5 min.

This film both harkens back to film's theatrical antecedents and presages later slapstick comedies. The office door of the camera-wielding sleuth/snoop identifies him as Hawkshaw the Detective, a popular figure who first appeared in the 1863 melodrama *The Ticket of Leave Man*. The jokes involving seltzer bottles and blackface derive from vaudeville and the music hall. Yet the film also rejoices in the newfound power of the moving picture camera: staging a car "accident" through stop-action and the substitution of dummy for actor, and placing the action in "real" cars, on "real" golf courses and aboard "real" boats, locations Sen-

nett and Chaplin would later find invaluable. Particularly fascinating, from a cinematic viewpoint, is the film's reflexive meditation on voyeurism and the punishment accorded the photographer and perhaps, by extension, filmmakers.

The narrative structure resembles that of many early films, relying upon a redundant situation to tie together various characters and locations. Throughout ten of the film's eighteen shots the detective tries to photograph an "illicit" couple and the film climaxes in the chase, popular in both comic and dramatic films of the time.

—Roberta E. Pearson

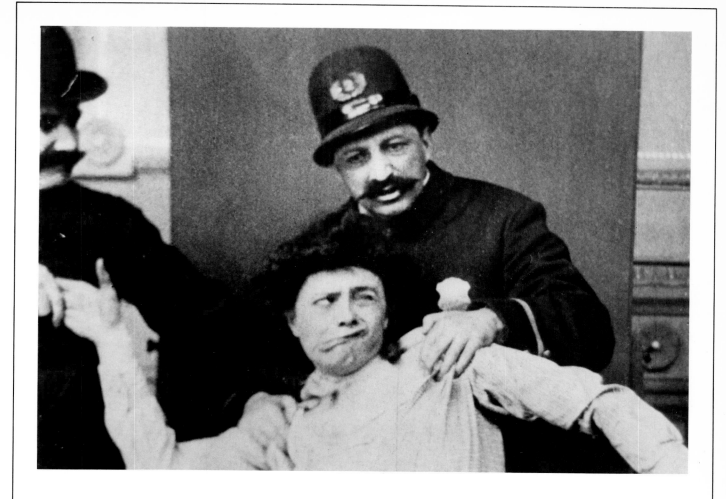

Photographing a Female Crook

© 2 February 1904. American Mutoscope and Biograph Company. Produced by Wallace McCutcheon. Photographed by A. E. Weed. Shot at Biograph's 14th Street studio, New York City on 13 January 1904. Print source: Library of Congress. 40 sec.

This brief film demonstrates two techniques—a medium close-up and a dolly-in camera movement—that those who maintain early cinema's devotion to primitive theatricality often claim did not exist until later. The story is slight, little more than an incident. A woman criminal, who is being forced to pose for her mug shot, responds by contorting her face, presumably so that the picture will be unrecognizable. In the first shot, while she is being held in place by police agents, the camera moves slowly toward her, enlarging her in order to emphasize her expressions. The second shot presents the actress in a medium close-up, smiling sweetly.

This film belongs to a genre popular during the period, based on facial expressions. The subjects were framed at the waist or closer so that their expressions could be clearly shown. Such close-ups were little more than a magical camera effect, an attraction of interest in itself. In later films, close-up shots play a narrative or psychological role, providing important story information or spectator empathy.

Biograph produced a number of films similar to this one, including *A Subject for the Rogues Gallery* (also filmed on 13 January 1904) and *Hooligan in Jail* (filmed by Billy Bitzer in 1903), which uses the same moving camera enlargement to show cartoon character Happy Hooligan eating a bowl of "prison hash" while behind bars. However, because the subject of *Photographing a Female Crook* is a woman, the film also relates to the erotic genre of early film. There was a fascination with seizing images of women in less than genteel situations. In this film, "she struggles to escape, and makes frightful grimaces, and in the struggle her waist is partly torn off. In the later part of the picture the face of the woman is shown full size" (original Biograph publicity bulletin, 1905). Seen in this context, the woman's struggle, the male hands steadying her, and the devouring gaze of the camera as it moves forward to catch the spectacle make this a classic film for feminist scholars.
                                                                    —Tom Gunning

The Black Hand

© 24 March 1906. American Mutoscope and Biograph Company. Produced by Frank Marion.
Photographed by G. W. Bitzer. With Robert Vignola and Anthony O'Sullivan. Shot at Biograph's 14th Street studio
and on Seventh Avenue, New York City on 15–16 March 1906. Print source: Museum of Modern Art. 7 min.

Typical of the pre-Griffith cinema, *The Black Hand* is shot
in long, static takes with no close-ups and only one pan.
In addition to the intertitles, there are only seven action
shots. The film tells an apparently true story of the abduc-
tion (and rescue) of a little girl by Italian thugs. Set in what
purports to be New York's Little Italy, the film is valuable in
capturing prevailing ethnic stereotypes at the turn of the
century. It is also noteworthy for the exterior shots of
horseless vans competing with horses, piles of dirty snow,
and curious passers-by staring at the still-novel motion
picture camera. The reality of these location shots clashes
dramatically with the artificiality of the studio scenes.

—Charles Silver

Terrible Ted

Released 25 September 1907. American Mutoscope and Biograph Company. Directed by Joseph Golden. Photographed by G. W. Bitzer. Filmed at Biograph's 14th Street studio, New York City, and the New York area. Print source: Museum of Modern Art. 9 min.

At the beginning of 1907, the Biograph Company's head of production, Frank Marion, left to form Kalem. Over the next year, Biograph worked with different directors including Joseph Golden whose *Tired Tailor's Nightmare* (1907) and *The Deaf-Mute Ball* (1907) are also extant. Eventually Golden went on to write scripts for David Horsely's Centaur and Nestor companies, and D. W. Griffith became Biograph's resident director.

Golden's *Terrible Ted* was part of the "bad boy" comedy subgenre that included Blackton and Smith's *Maude's Naughty Little Brother* (1900), Pathé's *Les Petits Vagabonds* (1905), Porter's *The Little Train Robbery* (1905) and *The Terrible Kids* (1906), and Biograph's *The Truants* (1907). The genre had found earlier expression in popular literature (*Peck's Bad Boy*) and comic strips ("The Katzenjammer

Kids"). Such film plots were abruptly abandoned in 1908 in response to public campaigns characterizing nickelodeons as "schools of crime" for their adult (and child) audiences. Ted only *dreams* his violent deeds, yet the film no doubt confirmed the reformers' worst fears: a child fantasizing about shooting police, holding up a stagecoach, and killing a band of Indians. A missing ending only made matters worse. When a nickelodeon opened on Staten Island, "*Terrible Ted* was the star film but unfortunately the moral was cut out either by design of the renter, or because he could not afford to buy the worn out piece; anyhow it is bad policy to leave the story finishing with only Ted displaying the scalps and not let the people know it was only a dream" (*Moving Picture World* [11 January 1908], p. 26).

—C. M.

Foul Play; or, A False Friend

© 15 December 1906. Vitagraph Company of America. With Lou Delaney and Florence Turner (?). Shot at Vitagraph's Flatbush, Brooklyn, studio and in surrounding area. Print source: George Eastman House. 10 min.

Vitagraph, a major American film company during the Nickelodeon era, excelled at producing contemporary dramas. *Foul Play* is the story of a wife who proves her husband's innocence by exposing his business associate as the real thief. The film's expansive sets were made possible by Vitagraph's new larger studio, completed in the fall of 1906. The pattern of composing in depth for interior scenes is established throughout the film; numerous shots contain actions transpiring on multiple planes, and the drama is played toward the center of the frame. The sequence in which the wife produces the evidence contains an extraordinary collision between film's old means of expression and the new, that is, between simultaneous action represented within the same shot on one hand, and across successive shots on the other. Many months before Griffith began directing at Biograph, Vitagraph films such as *The Hundred-to-One Shot; or, A Run of Luck* (1906), *Foul Play* (1907), and *The Mill Girl—A Story of Factory Life* (1907) had established the concept of parallel editing.   —Jon Gartenberg

The Thieving Hand

© 17 January 1908. Vitagraph Company of America. Shot at Vitagraph's Flatbush, Brooklyn, studio.
Print source: George Eastman House. 4 min.

Vitagraph's object animation used different trick effects, primarily in films involving the mix-up of dummies with real people. In *The Thieving Hand*, a one-armed man obtains an artificial limb. The man cannot control his new arm, which steals from passers-by. Stop-motion substitutions are used to interchange a dummy hand with a real one, and wires are used to pull the arm when it is detached from the rest of the body. In another film, *The Window Demonstration* (Vitagraph, 1907), the mannequins in the window are played by real people, who imitate staccato movements of mechanical dummies.

Both Vitagraph's founders, J. Stuart Blackton and Albert E. Smith, were interested in exploring the uses of animation and trick effects in film. Blackton's precinematic career was as a cartoonist and Smith's as a magician. Vitagraph's object animation films were seen by numerous filmmakers includ-

ing Frenchman Emile Cohl, and New York cartoonist Winsor McCay. Once they discovered Vitagraph's method, the technique was imitated, and improvements followed. Vitagraph's object animation films were the bridge between the stop-motion substitution films of Méliès and his contemporaries and the cartoons (animated drawing films) of later years.
—Jon Gartenberg

"The Thieving Hand" is a fine trick film, full of ingenuity and good quality. The closing scene spoils an otherwise perfect reproduction, where the convict receives again his arm and the poor pencil vendor goes free. No suspect is placed among convicts until he has had a trial. If the makers had shown a convict gang outside, instead of in the cell, the film would be perfect (*Moving Picture World* [1 February 1908], p. 72).

The Unwritten Law: A Thrilling Drama
Based on the Thaw-White Case

© 4 March 1907. Sigmund Lubin. Preserved by the National Film Archive. London.
Print source: Museum of Modern Art/National Film Archive, British Film Institute. 11 min.

The Unwritten Law is the kind of sensational film that the progressive forces of reform and uplift were eager to suppress in the nickelodeon era. Thanks to newspaper coverage, audiences were familiar with the lurid events and high life surrounding the murder of Stanford White by Harry K. Thaw on 25 June 1906, and they could more easily follow the film than we can today. In reality, the verdict of the court had not yet been delivered when this film was made. The reenactment illustrates the notorious events instead of telling the story. Each shot is complete in itself, and the relation of one shot to the next is only that of chronology.

The Unwritten Law was quite an ambitious production for its time, in the number of scenes, the variety of richly painted backdrops, and the special effects of the vision scenes. While in his prison cell, Thaw remembers his crime and his loved ones in a series of images that appear on the wall and dissolve from one to the next. —Eileen Bowser

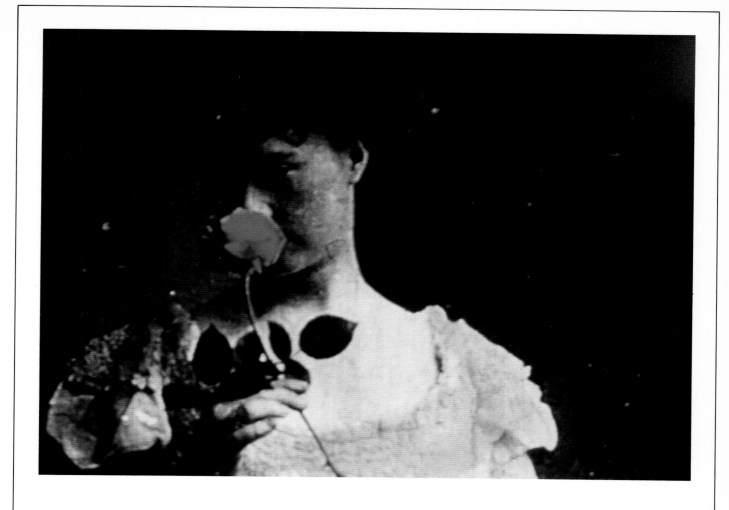

Three American Beauties

© 1 May 1906. Edison Manufacturing Company. Produced by Edwin S. Porter and Wallace McCutcheon. Photographed by Edwin S. Porter. Shot at Edison's 21st Street studio, New York City, on 17 March 1906. Print source: Museum of Modern Art. 40 sec.

This short film, which was usually tinted, was meant to be shown at the conclusion of an evening's program. So many prints were made of the popular film that its negative wore out, forcing Porter to reshoot *Three American Beauties* in September 1907. —C. M.

Program 3: America in Transition

A Tin-Type Romance (1910).

First Mail Delivery by Aeroplane

Released 17 October 1911. Powers. Shot at Aeroplane Postal Station 1, aviation field at
Nassau Boulevard, Long Island, New York. Print source: Library of Congress.
2.5 min.

"This reflects the future when a large portion of our mails
will be carried overhead in some such fashion as is
herein pictured. This film shows a 'regularly established'
U.S. Government Aeroplane Mail Station or post-office
with views of senders writing souvenir post-cards, sorting
the mail into the bag, placing the bag in the car, Captain
Beck, the first Government aeroplane mail carrier receiving
it, the start of the car and its ascension" (*New York Telegraph*
[22 October 1911], p. 4D).

Ancient Temples of Egypt

Released 12 October 1912. Kalem Company. Directed by Sidney Olcott. Photographed by George Hollister. With Gene Gauntier,
Jack Clark, Alice Hollister, J. P. McGowan, Robert Vignola, Doris Hollister, and George Hollister, Jr., and possibly Alan Farnum, "Philly" McDonald,
Sidney Olcott, Ameen Zatoun, or Abdullah Ya Fari. Shot at Luxor, Egypt, between January and March 1912. Print source: George Eastman House.
8 min.

In December 1911, the Kalem Company sent a filmmaking troupe to Egypt and Palestine; among the returns from the trip was this travelogue, in which the Kalem players give scale to the ruins at Karnak on the upper Nile. Nonfiction had been the dominant form of very early cinema, but by the teens, the popularity of storytelling had relegated subjects such as this one to the secondary function of "fillers," used to pad out the 1000-foot length that had become standard for reels of film.

Ancient Temples of Egypt, one of the infrequent actualities that Kalem produced, shared a reel with a burlesque com-edy. Yet this modest work is a powerful testament to the intrinsic and persistent allure of the documentary, offering scenes wonderfully uncontrived by movie artifice. And, unlike the prevailing stasis of the frame in fiction films, the camera is moved in 40 percent of these shots. In the final accounting, these brief views served as advance publicity for the other films that came out of Kalem's Middle Eastern expedition—most notably, one of the first American feature-length films, *From the Manger to the Cross* (1912), a Life of Christ enacted on "actual locations" in the Holy Land.
—Herbert Reynolds

Princess Nicotine; or, The Smoke Fairy

Released 10 August 1909. Vitagraph Company of America. Produced by J. Stuart Blackton. Photographed by Tony Gaudio.
Shot at Vitagraph's Flatbush, Brooklyn, studio. Print source: American Film Institute. 8 min.

Beginning with Méliès' work, trick films have fascinated audiences. *Princess Nicotine* provoked a full chapter in Frederick A. Talbot's *Moving Pictures: How They Are Made and Worked* (1912). Talbot describes how the illusion of a size disparity between the gentleman and the fairies was created: the actresses stood near the camera, their diminished reflections captured in a mirror positioned beyond the gentleman. Enlarged stage props, stop and reverse-motion cinematography, double-exposures, and editing completed the "cinematographic chicanery."

While there is a continued fascination today with special effects, from a modern perspective, *Princess Nicotine*, like so many other period comedies, also abounds in rather unsettling displays of slapstick and mildly violent confrontations between those of differing walks of life. Yet the *New York Dramatic Mirror* in 1909 described the character Princess Nicotine as "a charming young girl" who does "interesting acts to [the gentleman's] great amusement." In this regard, *Princess Nicotine* raises the troubling questions of what constitutes humor and satire and how the pleasurable can become unpleasurable, much as the gentleman's smoking habit turns on him.   —Janet Staiger

A Tin-Type Romance

Released 6 December 1910. Vitagraph Company of America. Directed by Larry Trimble. With Jean (the dog), Lou Delaney, and Florence Turner. Shot in the Brooklyn area. Print source: American Film Institute. 10 min.

Vitagraph was one of the three major America production companies of the early silent period. Because so few of its films are available, Vitagraph's reputation has languished in comparison to Biograph and Edison. *A Tin-Type Romance* is a good example of the hundreds of one-reel comedies made during the company's strong middle years.

By the time this film was produced, the important American film companies had each devised a variety of comic plot situations that had proved to be popular and, at the same time, adaptable to an apparently limitless number of remakes. One of these was the "courtship" comedy—a type that appeared so frequently throughout the early silent period that it stands out as a true subgenre of film comedy.

In formula comedies such as this it was a challenge to invent enough "comic bits" and plot twists to keep each film lively and original, without changing things so much that the production lost the identifiable "look" of the company that produced it. One of Vitagraph's responses to this challenge was Jean, the Vitagraph dog. Jean was owned by the film's

director, Larry Trimble, who brought her to the Vitagraph studio in 1909. Jean's big break probably came about as the result of a competitive decision by Vitagraph to counter a popular series of Pathé films which was then featuring a dog in the lead role.

Jean, like her co-stars Leo Delaney and Florence Turner, was an all-around performer who was equally adept at comedy and melodrama. The attribute most often displayed by her on the screen was a benevolent and superior intelligence that enabled her to save her human companions from the consequences of their own or someone else's character flaws. If Jean did not create this canine persona for the silver screen, she certainly was the first to embody it as an internationally known animal performer from a major film studio.

Notable technical qualities in this film are the confid use of close-up and medium-close shots and the fine rom tic "moonlight" effect in the scene with Florence Turn

—Patrick G. Loughi

A Friendly Marriage

Released 5 September 1911. Vitagraph Company of America. Directed by Van Dyke Brooke. With Earle Williams (Lord Frances Towne),
Lillian Walker (Lillian Cotton), Van Dyke Brooke (Lawyer). Shot at Vitagraph's Flatbush, Brooklyn, studio and nearby area.
Print source: American Film Institute. 15 min.

By the early teens, Vitagraph films had gained a reputation for their consistent originality and complexity. *A Friendly Marriage* demonstrates a sophisticated early use of techniques which would eventually become staples of the Hollywood film. It uses about twice as many shots (fifty-nine) as the average one-reeler of its day and manages to convey a relatively complex and lengthy double plot line: the rise and fall of a miner's daughter's fortunes on the one hand and her husband's attempts to support himself as a writer on the other.

The film's visual style is also striking. After the intertitle "Schemers," we see a shot staged in depth, with a realistic grouping of characters in the foreground—even at the expense of having one participant keep her back to the camera throughout—as well as a considerable vista beyond the large window. Later, the action of the heroine seeing her husband with the vicar's daughter is presented through a shot of her in a carriage, followed by one through the vicarage window—an early example of point-of-view framing without the binocular or keyhole maskings of very early narrative films. As the *Moving Picture World* commented, "It is all very romantic and told with a vim which does much to maintain the interest."

—Kristin Thompson

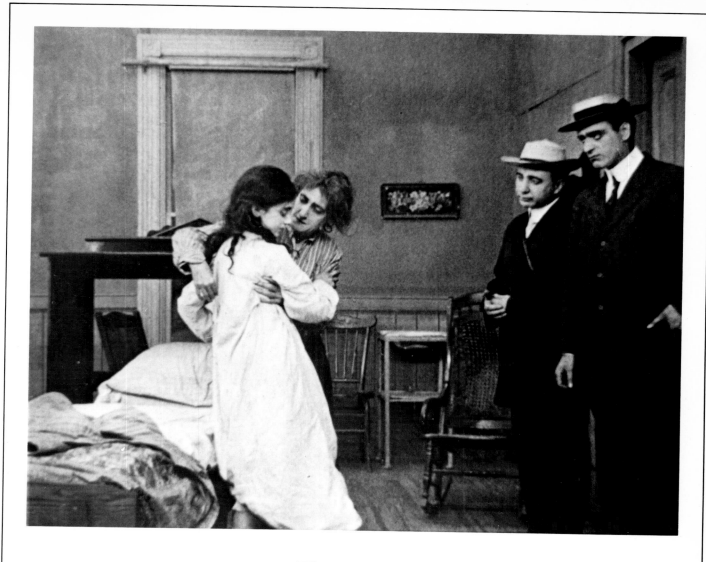

The Usurer

Released 15 August 1910. Biograph Company. Directed by D. W. Griffith. Scenario by D. W. Griffith. Photographed by George W. Bitzer
With George Nicholls (The Usurer), Grace Henderson (His Sister), Alfred Paget (A Collector), Anthony O'Sullivan (Another Collector), Kate Bruce
(Debtor), Henry Walthall (Debtor), Claire McDowell (Debtor). Shot at Biograph's 14th Street studio, New York City, on 10 and 15 July 1910.
Print source: Museum of Modern Art. 15 min.

Though there will always be claims and counter-claims for D. W. Griffith as an "inventor," it is an indisputable fact that his *use* of new filmmaking ideas was his greatest achievement. One of the least examined of his formal contributions to American films at the beginning of this century was his discovery of structures and atmospheres that echoed the subjects of his films.

Many of his Biograph films comment on social conditions, and the three strongest of these—*The Song of the Shirt* (1908), *A Corner in Wheat* (1909), and *The Usurer* (1910)—use an identical alternation of wealth/poverty, power/weakness, banquet/hunger. The clean cutting of the extreme contrasts makes the three films bold, early models of powerful film ideas and methods. The *New York Dramatic Mirror* greeted *The Usurer* as a "virile editorial in picture form." *The Usurer* also looks ahead to the complexities of *Intolerance* (1916).

—Jay Leyda

Winning an Heiress

Released 21 December 1911. Essanay Film Manufacturing Company. With John Steppling (Chauffeur). Shot at Essanay's Chicago studio and in surrounding areas during the fall of 1911. Print source: American Film Institute. 6 min.

John Steppling, one of America's forgotten silent comics, appeared in many Essanay films during 1911–12. At the time he enjoyed at least a modicum of acclaim. Likewise, Essanay had a well-deserved reputation for comedies well before Chaplin joined the company in 1915. *Winning an Heiress* received generally strong notices. —C. M.

"Novelty in theme is shown in this picture—comedy which will cause much laughter. Being very well put on and as creditably acted it is certain of success" (*New York Telegraph* [24 December 1911], p. 4D).

"A very amusing, yes, a delightful farce. It tells how an inpecunious young man took a course in automobiling at Chug's School, including instruction in running over a man, and then got a job as Mrs. Van Riche's chauffeur. It is very welcome" (*Moving Picture World* [6 January 1912]).

The Dream

Released 23 January 1911. Independent Moving Picture Company. Directed by Thomas Ince. Photographed by Tony Gaudio. Script by Mary Pickford. With Mary Pickford, Owen Moore, William Robert Daley, and Lottie Smith. Shot at IMP's New York studio. Print source: American Film Institute. 11 min.

Mary Pickford, remembered as America's Sweetheart, was one of the first stars of the screen. In December 1910, Carl Laemmle offered her $175 a week and successfully lured her from the Biograph Company where she starred in D. W. Griffith one-reelers. Laemmle also hired Owen Moore—to whom Pickford was secretly married—her brother Jack Pickford, sister Lottie Smith (later known as Lottie Pickford), and mother. Thomas Ince, who had been hired by Laemmle in October 1910, made a series of star-vehicle films featuring Little Mary. Pickford's first IMP film, *Their First Misunderstanding* was "a long story about jealousy on the part of a newly married couple" (*Moving Picture World* [25 January 1911], p. 182) and starred Pickford and Moore. *The Dream*, their second film, had a similar subject. It is hard to ignore the autobiographical aspects of the script: Moore's taste for alcohol was to be a major problem throughout their rocky marriage which finally ended in divorce. Although Ince only used two sets for this simply constructed film, Pickford's ability and range as an actress impresses modern audiences as strongly now as it did in 1911, when the reviewer for *Moving Picture World* called Mary, "The principal charm of the picture. . . . Our feelings, however, were somewhat sentimental when we saw 'our Mary' as a wife, arrayed in evening gown, and dining with swells. We felt the same misgivings that a father must feel when he observes his daughter as she stands upon the threshold of womanhood gazing into the new life to come. In other words, we have always considered 'Mary' as a child. It has never occurred to us that she might grow up and be a matron some day; but judging from her delineation of the matron, we have every reason to expect that her past experiences in portraying ingenue roles will be merely an epoch in her advancement and her final success as a leading woman" (25 January 1911, p. 182).

—C. M.

The Informer

Released 21 November 1912. Biograph Company. Produced and Directed by D. W. Griffith. Scenario by George Hennessy. Photographed by G. W. Bitzer. With Walter Miller (Confederate captain), Mary Pickford (his sweetheart), Henry B. Walthall (the false brother), Kate Bruce (Mother), Harry Carey (Union corporal) and Lionel Barrymore. Shot in Milford, Pennsylvania during October 1912. Print source: Library of Congress.

14 min.

The early American film industry produced many Civil War dramas between 1911 and 1915, as the country observed the fiftieth anniversary of that divisive, often familial conflict. For D. W. Griffith, the subject provided fertile ground for the development of narratives which could intertwine highly charged private and public emotions. Cowardice in the face of great danger was a device used before by Griffith in such Biograph releases as *The House With Closed Shutters* (1910) and *The Battle* (1911), but with *The Informer* he introduced the complicating element of duplicitous jealousy. George Hennessy, *The Informer*'s scenarist and one of Griffith's favored authors, expanded the context of sibling rivalry by placing it within the larger issue of sectional warfare. Griffith and his cameraman, G. W. "Billy" Bitzer, made striking use of their northeastern Pennsylvania location, offering landscapes and vistas which prefigure *The Birth of a Nation* (Biograph, 1915), but which also stand on their own as uncluttered and evocative settings. *The Informer* represents its director's most accomplished variation on the theme of family crisis during wartime until he began production on his epic drama less than two years later.

—Steven Higgins

Program 4: Domestic Life

One is Business; the Other Crime (1912).

The Old Actor

Released 6 May 1912. Biograph Company. Directed by D. W. Griffith. Scenario by George Hennessy. Photographed by G. W. Bitzer. With W. Chrystie Miller, Kate Bruce, Mary Pickford, Edwin August, Frank Opperman. Shot in California during February 1912. Print source: Library of Congress. 21 min.

In this delightful comedy from 1912, D. W. Griffith shows that his filmmaking was not limited to the click-clack editing of last-minute rescues, but could also develop a gentle comedy based on character. The leading player, W. Chrystie Miller, was a regular member of the Biograph acting company from 1909 on, playing elderly fathers, ministers, and Indian chiefs, and providing Griffith with a bit of individuality in minor roles. Here, however, Miller takes on one of his few leading roles as an out-of-work repertory actor who puts Shakespeare's adage, "All the world's a stage," to use by portraying a poor beggar to earn his daily bread.

But if this film does not use the dramatic parallel editing found in Griffith's melodramas, editing's potential to create a character to emphasize an idea is well demonstrated. In a series of four shots, Griffith cuts from a variety of camera positions, moving from long shot to close-up, to show the old actor's excitement on reading Shakespeare's claim that "men and women are merely players." We see a long shot of Miller reading on a porch. After an intertitle gives the Shakespeare quote we return to Miller, but now the shot of the old man is much closer, as if to convey his excitement over what he's reading. The next shot cuts to the daughter (played by young Mary Pickford) dancing inside the house, immediately showing the universality of performing. We then return to the close-up of Miller reading. This four-shot sequence unfolds naturally, and makes us more involved with the main character, as well as visually illustrating the idea contained in his reading. Likewise, later in the film the audition of the actor hired to replace Miller in the repertory company is intercut with Miller's "debut" on the street in his beggar makeup, revealing the acting involved in each action.

Its charm intact after seventy-five years, *The Old Actor* demonstrated Griffith's ability to construct comedy out of simple characters, using editing to provide insight into thoughts and motives, and lay the groundwork for an intellectual montage in which abstract ideas could be conveyed through the juxtaposition of images.

—Tom Gunning

The Passer-By

© 21 June 1912. Edison Manufacturing Company. Directed by Oscar C. Apfel. Scenario by Marion Brooks. Photographed by Henry Crongager and Otto Brautigan. With George Lessey (The Bridegroom), Miriam Nesbitt (His Mother), Marc MacDermott (The First to Pass). Shot at Edison's Bronx studio, 23–27 April and 7 May 1912. Print source: American Film Institute. 15 min.

The Passer-By illustrates one method of compressing a great deal of narrative action into the confines of a single reel: flashback structure. With the aid of a few dialogue titles, an entire life is revealed in ten minutes. Flashbacks were common enough in 1912, but here the device is cued by a surprising camera movement which directs our attention to the narrator and his story. Such shots were very rare, especially when used for more than informational purposes. When the studio staff had to describe this shot in preparing a release continuity, they had no word for it, and, borrowing a term used to describe panning shots in actualities, all they could say was, "panorama gets larger."
—Richard Koszarski

"Marion Brooks has written an ingenious scenario and the Edison Company has been at pains to give it adequate presentation. Marc McDermott is the leading figure in the play and his work is of the regular standard. There is some clever camerawork in the dinner scene when the machine is gradually pushed toward the speaker at the head of the table, and then withdraws. The effect, of course, is that of the actor being drawn toward the spectator and then receding. The stock exchange scene is unusually well-done. 'The Passer-By' is high class drama" (*Moving Picture World* [6 July 1912], p. 43).

The Water Nymph

Released 23 September 1912. Keystone Company. Produced and Directed by Mack Sennett. With Mack Sennett (Mack),
Mabel Normand (His Girlfriend), and Ford Sterling (His Father) Shot in Venice, California in late August or early September 1912.
Print source: UCLA Film Archives. 8 min.

In this short comic film, Mack Sennett choreographs a narrative that makes full use of his famous "bathing girls." Sennett plays a young man named "Mack" who is aware of his father's wandering eye. As a joke, he convinces his girlfriend (Mabel Normand) to flirt with the elderly man at the beach. In the comedy that ensues, the patriarch is seduced and abandoned, through the machinations of his son's grand oedipal prank. If, as some theorists have claimed, comedy frequently involves the degradation of the father, *The Water Nymph* is an early example in cinema of the classic strategy.

The film displays little of the physical slapstick humor that Sennett is known for in his Keystone Kops series. Rather, the comedy is based on characterization (the father's ridiculous posturing, the girl's mocking disdain) and on notions of mistaken identity and self-delusion. Finally, *The Water Nymph* makes clear the relation of comic structure to sexual difference, in its articulation of the male quest fantasy (humorously subverted), and in its play on the voyeuristic pleasure (within and without the narrative) of men watching women at the beach. Clearly, Sennett's biographer, Gene Fowler, saw the issue otherwise and cast the director as a virtual pioneer of women's liberation, one for whom, "if the ladies who unveil nineteen-twentieths of their bodies at our beaches knew that [he] was their deliverer from heavy raiment, they would rear statues to him at Atlantic City, Miami and other summer capitals" (Gene Fowler, *Father Goose* [New York: Covici Friede Publishers, 1934], p. 189).

—Lucy Fischer

"The only interest that one can find in this picture is in the diving Venus, who exposes her feeling so daringly. Perhaps that is just what the producer desires." (*New York Dramatic Mirror* [25 September 1912], p. 23).

One Is Business; the Other Crime

Released 25 April 1912. Biograph Company. Directed by D. W. Griffith. Scenario by George Hennessy.
Photographed by G. W. Bitzer. With Charles H. West (Poor Husband), Dorothy Bernard (Poor Wife), Edwin August (Rich Husband),
Blanche Sweet (Rich Wife), Kate Bruce (The Maid), and Robert Harron (Delivery Boy). Shot at the Biograph Company's California studio at
Georgia and Girard Streets, Los Angeles, in February 1912. Print source: Museum of Modern Art. 15 min.

A poor man, in desperation over his wife's illness, turns to robbery, and a rich man nonchalantly accepts a bribe. D. W. Griffith dramatically equates those actions; while the rich man's wife holds the would-be robber at gunpoint, she points out her husband's guilt: "He is no worse than you. . . . So. Yours is business; his is a crime."

To pave the way for this denouement, Griffith establishes a number of parallels between the two couples. Introducing them in their wedding finery at a moment when they "vow to follow the straight path," Griffith cross-cuts between the couples, presenting "poverty's desperation" (the poor woman in her sickbed) followed by views of the rich woman in her elegantly decorated home.

Griffith's "rhyming" use of windows reinforces the parallelism of the two settings: the poor woman gazes out her window as her husband leaves in search of work; the rich man sits by a window opening an envelope full of bribe money; ultimately, the poor man crawls through the rich man's window in an attempt to steal the ill-gotten gain.

Some of the most evocative images in the film feature the windows: curtains billowing in the breeze; sunlight streaming through windowpanes onto characters' faces. Griffith further differentiates between the "poor" and "rich" homes by treating the former with harsh, natural light and the latter with diffuse, electrical illumination, a point made most clearly as the wealthy man, sitting by a window and musing on his fate, flicks a light switch and is plunged into semi-darkness.

One Is Business; the Other Crime is enhanced by carefully selected exterior locations: a distant city framed by trees serves as a backdrop for the poor couple's futile efforts to make ends meet; the setting is later transformed by a gathering storm which lends emotional intensity to the film's ending. There are affecting performances by Dorothy Bernard and Blanche Sweet as women of different social classes who face formidable obstacles in their marriages rather than "live happily ever after."

—Janet K. Cutler

How Men Propose

Released 20 July 1913. Crystal. Print source: American Film Institute.
6 min.

How Men Propose is interesting because it presents men and marital rituals from the woman's subjective view. Already in love with another man, the heroine permits several men to propose to her as a ruse to deflect attention away from her real love. The scene is deliberately set up from the woman's perspective; various men enter the woman's room in order to propose, and the style each uses is ridiculed: the man's pomposity, arrogance, or timidity is offered as comic spectacle.

Made in 1913, when the suffragette movement was underway, and when women like Lois Weber, Cleo Madison, and E. D. Wilson were well-known directors, the film reflects a discourse not uncommon in these early Hollywood days. Man as object of woman's ridicule was apparently more acceptable than it was to be once the Hollywood classical system got fully underway.   —E. Ann Kaplan

"A little episode good for a laugh, presented at a straight forward manner and well acted" (*New York Dramatic Mirror* [23 July 1913], p. 32).

A House Divided

Released April 1913. Solax. Produced and directed by Alice Guy-Blaché. Filmed at the Solax Company studio, Fort Lee, New Jersey in April 1913. Print source: American Film Institute. 13 min.

When Alice Guy was secretary to Leon Gaumont, she went with him to see a demonstration of the Lumière brothers Cinématographe on 28 December 1895, at the Grand Café, Paris. So impressed was Gaumont, then a manufacturer of photographic equipment, that he began to mass-produce motion picture projectors and, in order to have films to feed through them, he arranged for "Mademoiselle Alice" to become the first woman producer/director of motion pictures. Her first release, *La Fée Aux Choux* (1896) was followed by hundreds of dramatic and comic subjects, 75 feet and later 150 feet in length, including the Gaumont Chronophone talking pictures.

She married cameraman Herbert Blaché and moved to Flushing, New York, in 1907 to run the Gaumont American distribution office. Forming her own corporation, the Solax Company, in 1910 with the help of two assistants and a business manager, she supervised the production of scores of romantic dramas, comedies, and motion pictures based on literary works, overseeing the details of each film much in the way Thomas Ince was to run his studio. *A House Divided*

represents the sort of concise story she was able to create for popular consumption using the simple chronological linking of shots to tell the story of a young couple who agree to live "separately together" after the husband accidentally gets the gum-chewing office stenographer's perfume on his clothing. In style and formula, *A House Divided* is a precursor of the scatter-brained domestic comedy epitomized by the "I Love Lucy" series on television.

—Audrey E. Kupferberg

"The story of the husband and wife who resolve not to speak to each other is given another lease on life. Here the two, after a little quarrel, communicate with each other by written notes. The piece flashes up as amusing for a moment or two, when the notes are shown on the screen, and then flickers out with a tame burglar scare—in reality only the hired girl getting in the cellar way. So explanations and kisses follow. Fair acting" (*New York Dramatic Mirror* [10 May 1913], pp. 30).

The Vampire

Released 15 October 1913. Kalem Company. Directed by Robert Vignola. Photographed by George Hollister.
With Harry Millarde (Harold Bentwell), Marguerite Courtot (Helen, his sweetheart), Alice Hollister (Sybil, the adventuress/vampire),
and Henry Hallam (Martin, Harold's employer); featuring Bert French and Alice Eis in their famous "Vampire Dance."
Shot at the Kalem studio in Cliffside, New Jersey in September 1913. Print source: George Eastman House. 38 min.

Popular imagination has long been filled with tales of sirens intent upon deterring the heroic odyssey of the male, but at the turn of this century, in response to the surge in feminism (demonstrably, in the demand for universal suffrage) the legendary vampire became a symbol for the aggressive seductress—the "vamp" as she would be called by the 1920s. The dance craze of the era cast this predator in the "vampire dance," one famous version of which provides the turning point in *The Vampire*. The elements in the film are the stock of melodrama, already exploited so effectively by D. W. Griffith: the beneficent life of the country and the pure sweetheart left behind are contrasted with the greater opportunities but graver evils of the city, personified by the temptress whose price is the potential destruction of the protagonist. Kalem's New York company filmed the vampire dance of a popular dance duo, Bert French and Alice Eis. (The elemental drama of their performance is oddly accentuated by the primitive realism of its surroundings, for though it is presented as occurring on-stage, it was actually photographed against a background of New Jersey for-

est—one curious result of Kalem's reliance on available light instead of studio illumination, further evidenced in the sun-drenched office "interior" elsewhere in the film.) The dance's inclusion in the film narrative causes the hero to recognize his fate, thus suggesting the morally redemptive capacity of theatrical art (and, by extension, of moving pictures, as Griffith had also implied in *The Drunkard's Reformation* [1909] and elsewhere). The power of *The Vampire*, however, lies not in a vehement sermon but rather in the sensationalism of its subject—and here it anticipates the pandering of DeMille—for its depiction of vice is far more commanding than its prescription of virtue. Theda Bara repeated the essence of this saga the following year in Fox's *A Fool There Was*.　　　　—Herbert Reynolds

"The acting of Miss Hollister as the adventuress in handling the different situations with the hero stands out. The director has carried detail to a fine point and very artistically. Photography good. J. C." (*New York Dramatic Mirror* [22 October 1913], p. 32).

Program 5: The Frontier Spirit

The Girl of the Golden West (1915).

The Girl of the Golden West (1915).

The Old West began to disappear just as the New West, meaning Hollywood, was establishing itself. Arizona, for example, did not become a state until 1913. Old and new overlapped, and the cowboys, wranglers, and ex-lawmen saw in the movies a way of extending their life style by a few more years (and, in the process, romanticizing it as well). The Hollywood Westerns were able to use not only these men, but the Wild West shows with all their livestock, costuming, and rolling stock, together with the still-rugged and undeveloped California terrain. The Westerns still being made in the East, with their unsuitable locations, exaggerated costuming, and often poor acting, showed the influence of the dime novel, and what the Easterner thought was the real thing. In the West, at least in terms of the *look* of the frontier, Hollywood was providing, nominally, the real thing since it was reflecting actuality rather than re-creating it. Had the art of film been a few years older and into more sophisticated feature-length films, we might have had a record of the disappearance of the Old West as valid as the depiction of the Depression in the early talkies of Warner Brothers.

Fortuitously, the right men were in the right place at the right time. Producer Thomas Ince (with a stable of directors that included Francis Ford) and especially his star-writer-producer William S. Hart, presented an on-screen frontier that was *pictorially* almost documentarian, but was dramatically and emotionally an evocation of the West that *should* have been. D. W. Griffith through the *excitement* of the Western further expanded his experiments in cross-cutting by exploiting the terrain of California and the possibilities of the climactic race to the rescue. Concurrently Cecil B. DeMille was presenting *his* version of the West in a number of films based on eastern plays and thus combining romanticism with actuality of setting. The American Western started in artifice and pantomime in the East, found reality and a rough poetry as the industry moved west, and then deviated into myth and fiction as the star system took over.
—William K. Everson

Maiden and Men

Released 4 November 1912. American Film Manufacturing Company. Directed by Allan Dwan.
With Pauline Bush (The Maiden), Jack Richardson (The Ranch Heavy), J. Warren Kerrigan (Disappointed Suitor),
and Louise Lester (Boss-lady on Ranch). Shot in Santa Barbara, California, on 12 October 1912. Print source: American Film Institute.
14 min.

The American Film Manufacturing Company, known as "The Flying A," quite literally manufactured one-reel parables at its Santa Barbara locations, developing melodrama out of moral dilemmas in stock fashion. Here, the eponymous maiden is Pauline Bush whose less-than-tragic flaw seems to lie in literacy, an ability which leads her to read romance novels and to pine for distant lovers. She heads for the seas and mountains, as the novel suggests, but makes it only as far as the nearest ranch, where she ruptures the male bonding among the cowpokes before she is sent packing back to papa. Returning home, she rips up the book with the fervor of a maenad.

An arguably antifeminist prejudice underlies this tale of the temptress lurking beneath the vanity of maidens suddenly aware of their power over men. This newfound knowledge is capture in a charming bit as Bush puts her hair up and preens. Sexual knowledge suddenly becomes self-knowledge—a trap for the unwary maiden. Her expulsion from the society represented by the ranch reflects the tension between rural and urban values found in the popular art of the era. The film also reveals an interesting anti-intellectual bias toward cinema's artistic cousin, the romance novel, whose effects were considered just as insidious as the cinema's. The moral stance of *Maiden and Men* is a finger-wagging response to the contemporary demand for responsible and virtuous movies.

—Karen Jaehne

"The American's leading woman, cast in the role of the frouzy backwoods maiden who pines for the romance of the world—for a lover to whisper sweet words to her—displays rare quality in character delineation, and the three leading men, though called upon to do very little, are more than acceptable" (*New York Dramatic Mirror* [30 October 1912], p. 33).

The Ruse

Released 14 July 1915. New York Motion Picture Company. Scenario by A. P. Johnson and Thomas H. Ince. Photographed by Robert Doeran. With William S. Hart (Bat Peters), Jack Davidson (John Folsom), Clara Williams (Mary Dawson), Fanny Midgely (Mrs. Dawson), Gertrude Claire (Mother Grady), Robert Kortman (A Gangster), and Shorty Hamilton (A Cowboy). Shot in Edenville, California, 8–20 April 1915. Print source: Library of Congress/Blackhawk Films. 28 min.

The Ruse comes at the end of a series of eighteen two-reel Westerns Hart made for Thomas H. Ince's New York Motion Picture Company in 1914–1915. These sturdy, carefully produced films established William S. Hart as a major star, enhanced Ince's standing in the marketplace and strengthened the Western as an industry genre.

Hart, trained in the legitimate theater, learned his film-making skills at the hand of master producer Ince, and that advantage is everywhere evident in *The Ruse*: the ample variety of sets to establish the western milieu contrasts with the economical but effective hint of a big city locale; the script is crafted with the precision of a good short story; skillful camera placement and editing dynamics help to mold the tumultuous gambling den confrontation into a powerful climax. "The final scenes," noted *Moving Picture World* on 17 July 1915, "depicting the single-handed gunfight are very stirring. This is stronger than the average picture of this type."

The Ruse is unique in Hart's canon in being as much a story of the plucky working girl as that of the classic Western hero, though his subsequent features would always center on an idealized woman. Most striking, perhaps, to modern sensibilities is the film's seamless union of a colorful West, already a land of fictive rather than realist dimensions, with the workaday world of the contemporary city, a myth-making sleight of hand that troubled neither audience, critic, nor filmmaker in pre–World War I America.

—Diane Kaiser Koszarski

The Girl of the Golden West

Released 4 January 1915. Jesse L. Lasky Feature Play Company. Directed by Cecil B. DeMille. Scenario by Cecil B. DeMille, based on the play by David Belasco. Photographed by Alvin Wyckoff. Art direction by Wilfred Buckland. Edited by Cecil B. DeMille. With Mable Van Buren (The Girl), Theodore Roberts (Rance), House Peters (Ramerrez), Jeanie Macpherson (Nina). Released by the Paramount Pictures Corporation. Print source: American Film Institute. 80 min.

One year almost to the day passed between Cecil B. DeMille's arrival in California as a neophyte filmmaker and the release of his seventh "personally directed" motion picture—*The Girl of the Golden West*. For DeMille, it was a year of exhilarating, tireless activity—physically constructing his fledgling film studio and artistically creating its first few features. DeMille's immediate financial success allowed him to pursue his dream: adopting New York theatrical producer David Belasco as his model, DeMille lovingly crafted a body of ambitious films which he considered real plays on the screen.

Early in that busy first year, the Lasky Company bought movie rights to ten Belasco plays, and DeMille picked the juiciest plums for himself, including *The Girl of the Golden West*, his second Belasco picture. Not content simply to base his films on Belasco's plots, DeMille used his profits to hire Broadway technicians who could reproduce the "look" of his mentor's stage works. Thus, the film version of *The Girl of the Golden West* greatly benefited from the efforts of art director Wilfred Buckland. Previously responsible for the scenic beauty and superb lighting of Belasco's plays, Buckland was one of the first theatrical designers brought west to work in Hollywood. As the film begins, extensive panning shots seem designed to celebrate Buckland's barroom set—its richly detailed verisimilitude and grand scale—as much as to advance the story line. With Buckland's help, and that of master cinematographer Alvin Wyckoff, DeMille was able to achieve the film's dramatic, firelit bedtime scenes and its climactic blizzard sequence. Ironically, when the same blizzard "set piece" was first presented on Belasco's stage, reviewers touted it as approximating the thrill of the cinema. *The Girl of the Golden West* stands as a testament to DeMille's determination to transport key elements of Belasco's stagecraft to the screen and to *transcend* the theater he so admired; in his autobiography he says, "Beyond Belasco's realism the stage could hardly go. . . . There the camera was needed."

—Sam McElfresh

Program 6: Love and Misadventure

Young Romance (1915).

Dreamy Dud: He Resolves Not to Smoke

1915. Essanay Company. Directed by Wallace A. Carlson.
Print source: American Film Institute/Library of Congress.
7 min.

Several industrial factors combined to make Chicago an environment conducive to the development of the animated cartoon. The city was home to newspapers that employed leading comic-strip artists such as the *Tribune*, advertising agencies that supplied commercial trailers (sometimes animated), and film studios. Sydney Smith, Andy Hettinger, and other Chicago cartoonists were quick to follow the example of Winsor McCay in adapting their comic creations for the screen. Charles Bowers of the *Tribune* would eventually become a producer of cartoons and a film comedian in his own right.

Wallace Carlson began drawing sports cartoons for the Chicago *Inter-Ocean* when he was fourteen. By 1915, ani-mated versions of Smith's "Old Doc Yak," George McManus's "The Newlyweds," and McCay's "Gertie" had created a demand for screen cartoons that Carlson and the Chicago Essanay studio were eager to exploit. *Dreamy Dud: He Resolves Not to Smoke* shows that Carlson's high-contrast graphic style preserved the linear comic-strip look that is typical of most early animation in America. The fantasy and "dream" plot show McCay's influence. Although the *Dreamy Dud* series continued until 1917, this title seems to be the only surviving example. In 1920, Carlson returned to film work as the animator for a screen version of Sydney Smith's strip, "The Gumps."

—Donald Crafton

Who Pays?
Episode Seven: "Blue Blood and Yellow"

Released 17 May 1915. Balboa Amusement Company. Distributed by Pathé Exchange. Directed by Harry Harvey. Scenario by Will M. Ritchey. With Ruth Roland and Henry King. Shot at the Balboa studio in Long Beach, California. Print source: UCLA Film Archives. 40 min.

Although the series or serial had been in existence since 1913, it was not until 1915 and the twelve-part *Who Pays?* that the genre was used for any form of social commentary. The concept behind *Who Pays?* is that of a "drama with a purpose," each episode asking an ethical or sociological question. Episode Seven poses the question of who pays when an heiress allows "class" to prejudice her judgment and marries an aristocratic wastrel rather than a science student with no ancestral background. Although Henry King does not receive directorial credit, he was involved to some extent in the direction of the series and also proved himself a competent actor opposite Ruth Roland (later to become known for her work in serials). *Who Pays?* was produced at the Balboa studios in Long Beach, California, where King was to commence his directional career that same year.

—Anthony Slide

Young Romance

Released 21 January 1915. Jesse L. Lasky Feature Play Company. Directed and produced by George Melford. Written by William C. deMille, based on a play by William C. deMille after a story, "Transients in Arcadia," by O. Henry. Photographed by Walter Stradling. Art direction by Wilfred Buckland. With Edith Taliaferro (Nellie Nolan), Tom Forman (Tom Clancy), Raymond Hatton (Jack, Tom's chum), Florence Dagmar (Lou, Nellie's chum), Ernest "Al" Gracia (Count Spagnoli), Charles Wells (The Motorman), and Mrs. Lewis McCord (The Landlady). Print source: UCLA Film Archives. 61 min.

"This production forever silences the claim that refined comedy cannot be conveyed via the screen. A more refined comedy has never been shown since the days of Molière. Moreover, it is American refined comedy. You do not have to extract and then study over bits of humor as you have to do with so many foreign comedies (even the best), but the humor of the thing hits you directly in the solar plexus. It is the sparkling, exuberant bubbling humor of our own country condensed and trebly distilled and an everlasting provocation to hearty laughter. Nobody is kicked in the rear (mirabile dictu), there is no trick-hose or seltzer bottle, nobody falls over himself or herself and there is positively no chase. Old-time motion picture men will wonder how a screen comedy can be constructed without these time-honored ingredients, but they will cease to wonder after they have seen 'Young Romance' " (*Moving Picture World* [6 February 1915], p. 532).

Photograph Credits

Photographs appearing in this catalogue are not to be reproduced or published in any manner or for any purpose without express permission in writing from the American Federation of Arts.

Original frame enlargements provided by individual photographers:

Jan-Christopher Horak (courtesy International Museum of Photography at George Eastman House): pp. 47 (bottom), 52 (top left and right), 59 (top), 60 (top right), 74 (bottom), 92–94, 101, 130, 131, 137.

Joyce E. Jesionowski (courtesy Museum of Modern Art): pp. 43, 47 (top left), 48 (bottom left and right), 54 (bottom), 55 (center right), 70 (bottom right), 77 (top right), 105, 116, 124, 125, 129, 132.

Patrick G. Loughney (courtesy American Film Institute and Library of Congress): pp. 2, 39, 40 (top), 42 (top and center right), 44–46, 47 (top right), 49, 51, 52 (center left), 54 (top right), 55 (top and bottom), 56 (top right), 57, 58 (bottom), 59 (bottom), 60 (top left), 61, 63, 65 (top and center), 66, 70 (top), 71 (left), 73, 76 (top and bottom), 77 (top left, center, and bottom), 79, 85–87, 95, 97, 100, 102–104, 106–115, 119, 121–123, 138–146, 149–151, 153, 155, 156, 160.

Charles Musser: pp. 55 (center left), 126, 133.

Kemp R. Niver: pp. 42 (top left), 70 (bottom left), 75, 117.

John Tirpak (courtesy UCLA Film, Television, and Radio Archives): pp. 64, 98, 148, 161, 162.

Photographs and frame enlargements from other sources:

Academy of Motion Picture Arts and Sciences: pp. 76 (center), 147, 159.

American Museum of the Moving Image: pp. 20, 21 (bottom), 22 (top, courtesy Bison Archives), 23, 24 (gift of William R. Bogert, photo by Berkey K & L), 25 (gift of William R. Bogert, photo by Earl Ripling), 26–29 (courtesy Bison Archives), 30 (top, lent by Glenn Ralston, photo by Sarah Wells), 30 (bottom, gift of Glenn Ralston, photo by Scott Bowron).

Q. David Bowers: pp. 13, 31–35, 36 (bottom).

John L. Fell: pp. 40 (right), 41, 42 (bottom left and right), 69.

International Museum of Photography at George Eastman House: pp. 58 (top), 74 (top), 78 (top), 88–91, 99, 118, 152.

Richard Koszarski: pp. 36 (top), 37.

Brooks McNamara: pp. 52 (center right and bottom), 53 (top), 56 (top left).

Museum of Modern Art/Film Stills Archive: pp. 14, 15 (top), 16–19, 21 (top), 22 (bottom), 40 (bottom left), 48 (top left), 54 (top left), 65 (bottom), 71 (right), 154, 157.

Charles Musser: front cover (courtesy Museum of Modern Art); pp. 53 (bottom, courtesy Bison Archives), 96 (courtesy Thomas A. Edison National Historic Site), 127, 128, 135, 136.

Philadelphia Museum of Art/The Alfred Stieglitz Collection: pp. 78 (bottom).

Rockland County Historical Society: p. 15 (bottom).

Bibliography

Allen, Robert C. "Vaudeville and Film, 1895–1915: A Study in Media Interaction." Ph.D. dissertation, University of Iowa, 1977.

Allister, Ray. *Friese-Greene: Close-up of an Inventor.* London: Marsland, 1948.

Amengual, Barthelemy. *"The Life of an American Fireman* et la naissance du montage," *Les Cahiers de la cinémathèque* no. 17 (Christmas 1975).

Baker, Larry, "A History of Special Effect Cinematography in the United States, 1895–1914." M. A. thesis, West Virginia University, 1969.

Balio, Tino, ed. *The American Film Industry.* Madison: University of Wisconsin Press, 1976.

Barnes, John. *The Beginnings of the Cinema in England.* New York: Barnes and Noble, 1976.

Barr, J. Miller. "Animated Pictures," *Popular Science Monthly* 52 (December 1897): 177–88.

Benfield, Robert. *Bijou Kinema: A History of Early Cinema in Yorkshire.* Sheffield, U.K.: Sheffield City Polytechnic, 1976.

Bessy, Maurice. *Louis Lumière, inventeur.* Paris: Prisma, 1948.

———. *Méliès.* Paris: Anthologie du cinéma, 1966.

———, and Lo Duca, Giuseppe. *Georges Méliès.* Paris: J. J. Pauvert, 1961.

Black, Alexander. "Photography in Fiction." *Scribner's* 18 (September 1895): 348–60.

———. "The Camera and the Comedy." *Scribner's* 20 (November 1896): 605–10.

Bowser, Eileen. "The Brighton Project: An Introduction." *Quarterly Review of Film Studies* 4 (Fall 1979): 509–38.

Bromhead, A. C. *Reminiscences of the British Film Trade.* Proceedings of the British Kinematograph Society, offprint no. 21. British Kinematograph Society, 1933.

Brownlow, Kevin. *The Parade's Gone By. . . .* New York: Knopf, 1969.

Burch, Noël, "Porter or Ambivalence," *Screen* 19 (Winter 1978–79): 91–105.

Card, James. "Problems of Film History." *Hollywood Quarterly* 4 (Spring 1950): 279–88.

Ceram, C. W. [Kurt Wilhelm Marek]. *Archaeology of the Cinema.* New York: Harcourt, Brace, 1965.

Chanan, Michael. *The Dream That Kicks.* London: Routledge and Kegan Paul, 1980.

Cinema and Bioscope Magazine, nos. 1–4, 1906–7.

Cook, Olive. *Movement in Two Dimensions.* London: Hitchinson, 1963.

Currie, Barton W. "The Nickel Madness." *Harper's Weekly* 51 (August 24, 1907): 1246–47.

Deslandes, Jacques. *Le Boulevard du cinéma.* Paris: Editions du cerf, 1963.

———. *Histoire comparée du cinéma.* Vol. 1, *De la cinématique au cinématographe, 1826–1896.* Tournai, Belg.: Tornai Casterman, 1968.

———, and Richard, Jacques. *Histoire comparée du cinéma.* Vol. 2, *Du cinématographe au cinéma.* Tournai, Belg.: Tornai Casterman, 1966.

Deutelbaum, Marshall A. "Process and Circularity in Primitive Film Narrative." Ph.D. dissertation, University of Rochester, 1978.

———, ed. *"Image" On the Art and Evolution of the Film.* New York: Dover, 1979.

Dickson, Antonia and Dickson, W.K.L. "Edison's Invention of the Kineto-Phonograph." *Century* 48 (June 1894): 206–14.

Dickson, W.K.L. *Biograph in Battle.* London: Fisher Unwin, 1901.

Dickson, W.K.L. and Dickson, Antonia. *History of the Kinetograph and Kinetophonograph.* 1895. Reprint. New York: Arno, 1970.

East, John M. "Looking Back—When Croydon Was the Film Capital of Great Britain." In *Film Review, 1977–78,* edited by F. Maurice Speed. London: W. H. Allen, 1977.

Fay, Arthur. *Bioscope Shows and Their Engines.* Tarrant Hinton, U.K.: The Oakwood Press, 1966.

Fell, John L. *Film and the Narrative Tradition.* Norman, Okla.: University of Oklahoma Press, 1974.

———. "L'Articulation des rapports spatiaux." *Les Cahiers de la cinémathèque* 29 (Winter 1979): 81–87.

Fielding, Ray. *A Technological History of Motion Pictures and Television.* Berkeley: University of California Press, 1967.

Forty Years of Film History, 1895–1935: Notes on the Films. London: British Film Institute, n.d.

Frazer, John. *Artificially Arranged Scenes: The Films of Georges Méliès.* Boston: G. K. Hall, 1979.

Gartenberg, Jon. "Camera Movement in Edison and Biograph Films, 1900–1906." *Cinema Journal* 19 (Spring 1980): 1–16.

Gaudreault, André. "Detours in Film Narrative: The Development of Cross-Cutting." *Cinema Journal* 19 (Fall 1979): 39–59.

Gessner, Robert, "The Moving Image." *American Heritage* 11 (April 1960): 30–35.

Gifford, Denis. *The British Film Catalogue, 1895–1970.* Newton Abbot, U. K.: David and Charles, 1973.

Grau, Robert. *The Business Man in the Amusement World.* New York: Broadway, 1910.

_____. *Theater of Science*. New York: Broadway, 1914.

Gunning, Tom. "Le Style non-continu du cinéma des premiers temps." *Les Cahiers de la cinémathèque* 29 (Winter 1979): 24–34.

Haas, Robert Bartlett. *Muybridge: Man in Motion*. Berkeley: University of California Press, 1976.

Hagan, John. "L'Erotisme des premiers temps." *Les Cahiers de la cinémathèque* 29 (Winter 1979): 72–79.

_____. "Les Actions simultanées." *Les Cahiers de la cinémathèque* 29 (Winter 1979): 34–40.

Hamilton, Harlan. "Les Allures du cheval: Representées par la photographie instantanée." *La Nature*, December 14, 1897.

Hammond, Paul. *Marvelous Méliès*. New York: St. Martin's, 1975.

Hampton, Benjamin B. *A History of the Movies*. 1931. Reprint. New York: Dover, 1970.

Hendricks, Gordon. *The Edison Motion Picture Myth*. Berkeley: University of California Press, 1961. Reprint. New York: Arno, 1972.

_____. "A New Look at an Old Sneeze." *Film Culture* no. 22–23 (1961): 90–95.

_____. *Beginnings of the Biograph*. 1964. Reprint. New York: Arno, 1972.

_____. *The Kinetoscope: America's First Commercially Successful Motion Picture Exhibitor*. New York: The Beginnings of the American Film, 1966.

_____. *Eadweard Muybridge: The Father of the Motion Picture*. London: Secker and Warberg, 1975.

Hepworth, Cecil M. "Those Were the Days." In *The Penguin Film Review* 6 (1948): 33–39.

_____. *Came the Dawn: Memories of a Film Pioneer*. London: Phoenix House, 1951.

_____. *Animated Photography: The ABC of the Cinematograph*. 1900. Reprint. New York: Arno, 1970.

Hepworth, Thomas Cradock. *The Book of the Lantern*. 1899. Reprint. New York: Arno, 1978.

Holman, Roger, comp. *Cinema 1900/1906: An Analytical Study by the National Film Archive (London) and the International Federation of Film Archives*. 2 vols. Brussels, Belgium: Fédération Internationale des Archives du Film, 1982. Vol. 1: *Brighton Symposium, 1978*. Vol. 2: *Analytical Filmography (Fiction Films), 1900–1906*.

Hopkins, Albert A. *Stage Illusions and Scientific Diversions*. 1897. Reprint. New York: Benjamin Blom, 1967.

Hopwood, Henry V. *Living Pictures*. 1899. Reprint. New York: Arno, 1970.

Huettig, Mae D. *Economic Control of the Motion Picture Industry*. Philadelphia: University of Pennsylvania Press, 1944.

Hulfish, David. *The Motion Picture: Its Making and Its Theater*. Chicago: Electricity Magazine Corporation, 1909.

_____. *Cyclopedia of Motion-Picture Work*. Chicago: American School, 1911.

_____. *Motion Picture Work*. Chicago: American School, 1913.

"An Interview with J. Stuart Blackton." *The Moving Picture World*, December 19, 1908.

Jenkins, C. Francis. *Picture Ribbons*. Washington, D.C.: H. L. McQueen, 1897.

Jenkins, Charles Francis and Depue, Oscar B. *Handbook for Motion Picture and Stereopticon Operators*. Washington, D.C.: Knega, 1908.

Jenkins, Reese V. *Images and Enterprise: Technology and the American Photographic Industry, 1839–1925*. Baltimore: Johns Hopkins, 1975.

Jobes, Gertrude. *Motion Picture Empire*. Hamden, Conn.: Archon, 1966.

Jowett, Garth. *Film: The Democratic Art*. Boston: Little, Brown, 1975.

Lahue, Kalton C., ed. *Motion Picture Pioneer: The Selig Polyscope Company*. South Brunswick, N.J.: A. S. Barnes, 1973.

Levy, David. "The 'Fake Train Robbery': Les Reportages simulés, les reconstitutions et le film narratif américain." *Les Cahiers de la cinémathèque* 29 (Winter 1979): 42–56.

Leyda, Jay. *Kino*. London: Allen and Unwin, 1960.

Low, Rachel. *The History of the British Film, Vol. 2, 1906–1914*. London: Allen and Unwin, 1949.

_____, and Manvell, Roger. *The History of the British Film, 1806–1906*. London: Allen and Unwin, 1948.

MacDonell, Kevin. *Eadweard Muybridge: The Man Who Invented the Motion Picture*. Boston: Little, Brown, 1972.

"Making the First Picture Play." *Harper's Weekly* 38 (October 13, 1894).

Malthête-Méliès, Madeleine. *Méliès l'enchanteur*. Paris: Hachette, 1973.

Marey, Etienne Jules. *Movement*. 1895. Reprint. New York: Arno, 1970.

_____. "The History of Chronophotography." *Smithsonian Institution Annual Report for 1901*. Washington, D.C.: Smithsonian Institute, 1902.

Matthews, Brander, "The Kinetoscope of Time." *Scribner's* 18 (December 1895): 733–44.

May, Lary Linden. "Reforming Leisure: The Birth of Mass Culture and the Motion Picture Industry, 1896–1920." Ph.D. dissertation, University of California, Los Angeles, 1977.

_____. *Screening the Past: The Birth of Mass Culture and the Motion Picture Industry*. New York: Oxford University Press, 1980.

Mitry, Jean. *Histoire du cinéma. Vol. 1*. Paris: Editions universitaires, 1967.

Moving Picture World, 1907–27.

Musser, Charles. "The Early Cinema of Edwin Porter." *Cinema Journal* 19 (Fall 1979): 1–38.

Muybridge, Eadweard. *Muybridge's Complete Human and Animal Locomotion: All 781 Plates from the 1887 Animal Locomotion*. New York: Dover, 1979.

Niver, Kemp R. *In the Beginning: Program Notes to Accompany One Hundred Early Motion Pictures*. New York: Brandon Books, n.d.

_____. *Motion Pictures from the Library of Congress Paper Print Collection: 1894–1912*. Berkeley: University of California Press, 1967.

_____. *The First Twenty Years: A Segment of Film History*. Los Angeles: Locare Research Group, 1968.

_____. ed. *Biograph Bulletins, 1896–1908*. Los Angeles: Locare Research Group, 1971.

Optical Lantern and Cinematograph Journal 1–4 (1904–7). Sometimes published as *Kinematograph Journal: Incorporating Lantern Weekly*.

Optical Magic Lantern Journal 1–12 (1889–1903).

"Our Visits." *The Moving Picture World*, February 1, 1908.

Patterson, Joseph Medill. "The Nickelodeons," *Saturday Evening Post*, November 23, 1907. Anthologized in *The Saturday Evening Post Treasury*, edited by Roger Butterfield. New York: Simon and Schuster, 1954.

Paul, Robert W., Hepworth, Cecil M., and Barker, W. G. *Before 1910: Kinematograph Experiences*. Proceedings of the British Kinematograph Society, offprint no. 38. British Kinematograph Society, 1936.

Perry, George. *The Great British Picture Show*. New York: Hill and Wang, 1974.

Pierce, Lucy France. "The Nickelodeon." *The World To-Day* 15 (October 1908): 1052–57.

Pratt, George C. *Spellbound in Darkness: A History of the Silent Film*. Greenwich, Conn.: New York Graphic Society, 1966.

Projection Lantern and Cinematograph, nos. 1–12 (May 1906–September 1907).

Quigley, Jr., Martin. *Magic Shadows*. Washington, D.C.: Georgetown University Press, 1948.

Ramsaye, Terry. *A Million and One Nights*. 1926. Reprint. New York: Simon and Schuster, 1964.

Richardson, F. H. *Motion Picture Handbook*. 1910. New York: The Moving Picture World, 1910.

Robinson, David. *Origins of the Cinema: Catalogue of an Exhibition Presented by Cumberland Row Antiques Limited, July–August 1944*. London: Cumberland Row Antiques Limited, 1964.

Sadoul, Georges. "English Influence on the Work of Edwin S. Porter." *Hollywood Quarterly* 3 (Fall 1947): 41–50.

_____. *Histoire générale du cinéma*. Vol. 2, *Les Pionniers du cinéma: De Méliès à Pathé, 1897–1909*. Paris: Les Editions Denoël, 1947.

_____. *British Creators of Film Technique*. London: British Film Institute, 1948.

_____. *Histoire générale du cinéma*. Vol. 1, *L'Invention du cinéma, 1832–1897*. Paris: Les Editions Denoël, 1948.

_____. *Louis Lumière*. Paris: Editions Seghers, 1964.

_____. *Histoire du cinéma mondial: Des origines à nos jours*. Paris: Flammarion, 1968.

_____. *Georges Méliès*. Paris: Editions Seghers, 1970.

_____. *French Film*. 1953. Reprint. New York: Arno, 1972.

Salt, Barry. "Film Form, 1900–1906." *Sight and Sound* 47 (Summer 1978): 148–53.

Sklar, Robert. *Movie-Made America*. New York: Random House, 1975.

Slide, Anthony. *Early American Cinema*. New York: A. S. Barnes, 1970.

Sopocy, Martin. "A Narrated Cinema: The Pioneer Story Films of James A. Williamson." *Cinema Journal* 18 (Fall 1978): 1–28.

Spehr, Paul C. "Some Still Fragments of a Moving Past." *The Quarterly Journal of the Library of Congress* 32 (January 1975): 33–50.

_____. *The Movies Begin: Making Movies in New Jersey, 1887–1920*. New York: Newark Museum and Morgan and Morgan, 1977.

_____. "Filmmaking at the American Mutoscope and Biograph Company, 1900–1906." *The Quarterly Journal of the Library of Congress* 37 (Summer-Fall 1980): 413–21.

Spottiswoode, Raymond. "The Friese-Greene Controversy: The Evidence Reconsidered." *Quarterly of Radio, Film and Television* (Spring 1955).

Talbot, Frederick Arthur. *Moving Pictures: How They Are Made and Worked*. Philadelphia: J. B. Lippincott, 1912.

Thomas, David B. *The Origin of the Motion Picture: An Introductory Booklet on the Pre-History of the Cinema*. London: Her Majesty's Stationery Office, 1964.

Trutat, Eugène. *La Photographie animée*. Paris: Gauthier-Villars, 1899.

Vardac, A. Nicholas. *Stage to Screen: Theatrical Methods from Garrick to Griffith*. Cambridge, Mass.: Harvard University Press, 1949.

Walls, Howard Lamarr. *Motion Pictures, 1894–1912*. Washington, D.C.: Library of Congress, 1953.

Walsh, George Ethelbert. "Moving Picture Drama for the Multitude." *The Independent* 64 (February 6, 1908): 306–10.

Waters, Theodore. "Out with a Moving Picture Machine." *Cosmopolitan* 40 (January 1906).

Wenden, D. J. *The Birth of the Movies*. New York: Dutton, 1975.

Index